GRAMMAR AND BEYOND

WORKBOOK

Kerry S. Vrabel

1

CAMBRIDGE
UNIVERSITY PRESS

CAMBRIDGE UNIVERSITY PRESS
Cambridge, New York, Melbourne, Madrid, Cape Town,
Singapore, São Paulo, Delhi, Tokyo, Mexico City

Cambridge University Press
32 Avenue of the Americas, New York, NY 10013-2473, USA

www.cambridge.org
Information on this title: www.cambridge.org/9780521279888

First published 2012

Printed in the United States of America

A catalog record for this publication is available from the British Library.

ISBN 978-0-521-14293-9 Student's Book 1
ISBN 978-0-521-14304-2 Student's Book 1A
ISBN 978-0-521-14307-3 Student's Book 1B
ISBN 978-0-521-27988-8 Workbook 1
ISBN 978-0-521-27989-5 Workbook 1A
ISBN 978-0-521-27990-1 Workbook 1B
ISBN 978-1-107-69431-6 Teacher Support Resource Book with CD-ROM 1
ISBN 978-0-521-14330-1 Class Audio CD 1
ISBN 978-1-139-06183-4 Writing Skills Interactive 1

Art direction and layout services: TSI Graphics

Contents

PART 6 Simple Past

PART 7 More About Nouns, Determiners, and Pronouns

PART 12 Modals 2

PART 13 Adjective and Adverbs – Comparisons

Art Credits

Illustration

John Kurtz: 14, 17 (inset), 35, 68, 159, 223, 225; **Edwin Fotheringham:** 22, 63, 113, 131, 137 (b), 148, 155, 156 (t), 184; **Pat Byrnes:** 29, 37, 50, 106, 122, 128, 130, 132, 150, 177 (t), 216; **Andrew NG:** 34, 98, 120, 121, 136, 137 (t), 156 (b), 173; **Foo Lim:** 36, 56 108, 124, 177 (b), 194, 208, 218

Photography

2 ©iStockphoto.com/Stalman; 4 (l) ©iStockphoto.com/2HotBrazil, (c) ©iStockphoto.com/Brosa, (r) ©iStockphoto.com/PacoRomero; 8 Tetra Images/Getty Images; 9 (l) Commercial Eye/Getty Images, (c) Kablonk!/Photolibrary, (r) Uppercut Images/Getty Images; 45 (t) Richard Nowitz/Getty Images, (b) ©iStockphoto.com/inhauscreative; 46 Danita Delimont/Getty Images; 53 Masterfile Royalty Free; 54 David Hiser/Getty Images; 57 ©iStockphoto.com/Dougall Photography; 60 Gardel Bertrand/Photolibrary; 62 Siri Stafford/Getty Images; 70 Liquid Library/Thinkstock; 74 NASA; 76 Bloomberg/Getty Images; 77 ©iStockphoto.com/Dorling Kindersley; 84 Rick Friedman/Corbis; 85 Bjoern Sigurdsoen/epa/Corbis; 86 Inti St Clair/Blend Images/Corbis; 88 ©iStockphoto.com/ma-k; 90 Redferns/Getty Images; 91 AFP/Getty Images; 93 2011 Anchorage Museum, B76.40.9/AlaskaStock.com; 104 Noel Hendrickson/Getty Images; 143 Fabio Cardoso/Corbis; 164 Charles Christian Nahl/Corbis; 171 Barry Lewis/In Pictures/Corbis; 176 Courtesy of www.tastebudscook.com; 179 Stockbyte/Thinkstock; 185 ©Helder Almeida*; 187 Mark Scott/Getty Images; 188 Condé Nast Archive/Corbis; 195 ©iStockphoto.com/bo1982; 201 Creatas Images/Thinkstock; 214 Hemera/Thinkstock; 222 ©Colin D. Young*; 230 ©Diane N. Ennis*; 232 ©iStockphoto.com/FabioFilzi; 236 Frans Lanting/Corbis

*2011 Used under license from Shutterstock.com

UNIT 1

Statements with Present of *Be*

Tell Me About Yourself

Present of *Be*: Affirmative Statements

1 Complete the sentences with *am*, *is*, or *are*. Use the full forms.

My name is Tasha, and I __*am*__ from Poland. I _____ a student
                        (1)   (2)

at Parkview University. It _____ a good school. My major _____
                          (3)   (4)

chemistry. I _____ a senior this year. My sister Anka _____ at
             (5)   (6)

Parkview, too. She _____ 19 years old. Her favorite subjects _____
                   (7)   (8)

computer science and art. Our grades _____ very good. My mother
                                     (9)

and father _____ in Poland. They _____ professors at the college
           (10)   (11)

in our hometown. They _____ happy we are at a good university.
                      (12)

2 Complete the conversation with *'m*, *'re*, or *'s*.

Tasha: Hi. I __*'m*__ Tasha.
                 (1)

José: Hi, Tasha. I _____ José. I _____ from Colombia.
                       (2)   (3)

Tasha: I _____ Polish.
            (4)

José: You _____ in my English class. My friend Yuchin is in our class, too. She _____
              (5)   (6)

Chinese. Oh, and my friend Juan is in our class, too. He _____ from Ecuador.
                                                         (7)

Tasha: The class is very international! My major is chemistry. It _____ very interesting.
                                                                     (8)

José: My major is chemistry, too. Maybe we _____ in the same classes.
                                               (9)

Tasha: Maybe! They _____ big classes. My sister Anka is in our English class, too.
                       (10)

She _____ a computer science major.
    (11)

José: You _____ both science majors?
              (12)

Tasha: Yes, and our parents are happy about that. They _____ chemistry and engineering
                                                          (13)

professors in Poland.

José: You _____ from a very scientific family!
              (14)

3 Complete the sentences with the subject pronouns *I, you, he, she, it, we,* and *they* and the verbs *am, is,* or *are.* Use the full forms.

A   **Kent Community College** is very well-known. ____It____ ____is____ in New York.
(1)   (1)

_____ _____ more than 50 years old. **The students** are from different countries.
(2)   (2)

_____ _____ all interesting.
(3)   (3)

B   **I** am a student at Kent Community College. _____ _____ a business major.
(4)   (4)

My major is very interesting. _____ _____ a popular major for many students.
(5)   (5)

My friend Michael is a business major, too. _____ _____ from Australia.
(6)   (6)

Michael and I are good friends. _____ _____ in all of the same business classes.
(7)   (7)

C   **My sister, Susan,** is at Kent Community College, too. _____ _____ a music
(8)   (8)

major. **Her instruments** are piano and guitar. _____ _____ easy for her. **Susan**
(9)   (9)

and I are singers. _____ _____ in the school chorus.
(10)   (10)

D   **You and your classmates** are students, too. _____ _____ in an English class.
(11)   (11)

_____ _____ ready to improve your English.
(12)   (12)

4 Unscramble the words to make sentences. Use *am, is,* or *are.*

1. a business major / Jack   *Jack is a business major.*_____

2. His school / in Florida   _____

3. very popular / It   _____

4. right now / in class / He   _____

5. Rita / His sister   _____

6. 18 years old / She   _____

7. His friends / good students   _____

8. accounting majors / They   _____

9. I / an English student   _____

10. English students / You and José   _____

5 Write sentences that are true about you. Use *am*, *is*, or *are*.

1. I (occupation)   *I am a student.*_____

2. I (nationality)   _____

3. My teacher (nationality)   _____

4. My classes (difficult/easy)   _____

5. My favorite subject (class subject)   _____

Present of *Be*: Negative Statements

1 Complete the sentences. Use *am not*, *is not*, or *are not*.

1. Boston is a big city. It _is not_ in the state of New York.

2. Many buildings in Boston are old. They _____ new.

3. The weather in this city is cold in the winter. It _____ warm.

4. Los Angeles is a very popular city. It _____ a boring city.

5. The people in Los Angeles are from many countries. They _____ all from the United States.

6. We are students. We _____ teachers.

7. You are in an English class. You _____ in a Spanish class.

8. I am from Boston. I _____ from Los Angeles.

9. My friend Lisa is a math teacher in Boston. She _____ a science teacher.

10. Daniel is an English teacher in Boston. He _____ a French teacher.

11. Daniel and Lisa _____ teachers in the same school.

12. Lisa _____ in the English department.

2 A Look at the student ID cards. Write sentences with *'s not* and *'re not* after pronouns and *isn't* and *aren't* after names and nouns.

GC Green College
Student ID Card

Gena Mohamed
Date of Birth: June 16, 1992
Nationality: Iraqi
Major: Mathematics

FV *Fox Valley College*
Student ID Card

Noor Hamed
Date of Birth: May 14, 1990
Nationality: Kenyan
Major: Business

GC Green College
Student ID Card

Mei Chow
Date of Birth: July 6, 1992
Nationality: Chinese
Major: Computer science

1. Gena Mohamed / from Egypt

   Gena Mohamed isn't from Egypt.

2. Noor Hamed / 36 years old

   _____

3. His major / computer science

   _____

4. Noor / Iraqi

   _____

5. Gena and Mei / at Fox Valley College

   _____

6. They / business majors

   _____

7. Mei / Kenyan

   _____

8. Gena, Noor, and Mei / teachers

   _____

B Write your own sentences about Gena, Noor, and Mei. Write affirmative sentences with *is* and *are*. Then write negative sentences with *'s not* and *'re not* after pronouns and *isn't* and *aren't* after names and nouns. Use the information from the ID cards.

Affirmative

1. *Gena is from Iraq.* _____

2. _____

3. _____

4. _____

Negative

5. *Gena and Noor aren't computer science majors.* _____

6. _____

7. _____

8. _____

Avoid Common Mistakes

1 Circle the mistakes.

1. Sarah **is** a student. She **is** ⟨**no**⟩ in class now. She **is** in the library.
   (a)　　　　　　　　(b)　　　　　　(c)

2. **Alex and Mary academic advisers.** They **are** always busy. They **are** helpful.
   (a)　　　　　　　　　　　　　　　(b)　　　　　　　　(c)

3. Mr. Garcia **is** a teacher. His classes **are** interesting. **Is** a good teacher.
   (a)　　　　　　　　　　(b)　　　　　　(c)

4. My major **is** education. **Is** a popular major. Many students **are** interested in it.
   (a)　　　　　(b)　　　　　　　　　　　(c)

5. Susan **is** my roommate. **We** the same age. We **are** 19 years old.
   (a)　　　　　　(b)　　　　　　(c)

6. The computers **are** in the library. They **are** old. They **are no** new.
   (a)　　　　　　　　(b)　　　　　　(c)

7. You **are** in my English class. **I** always late. You **are** always on time.
   (a)　　　　　　　　(b)　　　　　　(c)

8. I **am** crazy about science. My major **is** biology. I **am no** interested in business.
   (a)　　　　　　　　　　(b)　　　　　　(c)

2 Find and correct eight more mistakes in the university tutoring program's website.

○ ○ ○   ▭

Hope University   Learning Center: Tutoring Service

are
Welcome to the Learning Center. Our tutors ^ here six days a week. The center is no open on

Sunday. Is in the building next to the library. The hours are from 8:00 a.m. to 8:00 p.m. The service

free. It is no difficult to use. Appointments necessary. All tutors are graduate students at the

university. They are no professors. They are very helpful. They are smart and friendly. Your grades

important to us. Students are always happy with our service, and we happy to help you!

Self-Assessment

Circle the word or phrase that correctly completes each sentence.

1. Sandra and I _____ at Metro Community College.

   a. am students　　　b. aren't students　　　c. students

2. _____ are in the library.

   a. She　　b. It　　c. You

3. John is a psychology major. _____ 21 years old.

    a. It is   b. He is   c. Is

4. _____ in class now.

    a. They   b. They are   c. They be

5. The adviser _____ interested in my academic plans.

    a. are   b. is   c. no is

6. Pedro is good with computers. _____ a music student.

    a. He   b. He isn't   c. I no am

7. I _____ 21 years old.

    a. is   b. am   c. are

8. My business class is fun. _____ boring.

    a. It's not   b. It aren't   c. It no is

9. We are good students. _____ late for class.

    a. We no are   b. We're not   c. We no

10. The English class is at 1:00 p.m. _____ at 2:00 p.m.

    a. It no   b. No is   c. It's not

11. Brian _____ late for class today.

    a. are   b. is no   c. is

12. Sara and James are at the movies. _____ at the library.

    a. They are not   b. He is not   c. She is not

13. Anna and I are in the same classes. _____ both on the soccer team, too.

    a. She is   b. They are   c. We are

14. The computers in the classroom _____ very good.

    a. is not   b. are no   c. are not

15. The students _____ adults.

    a. are   b. is   c. isn't

2

Yes/No Questions and Information Questions with *Be*

Schedules and School

Yes / No Questions and Short Answers with *Be*

1 Yolanda meets John in the registration office. Complete her questions with *am*, *is*, or *are*. Then give John's short answers.

1. **Q:** ___*Are*___ we in the registration building?   **A:** Yes, _____*we are*_____ .

2. **Q:** _____ I late for registration?   **A:** No, _____ .

3. **Q:** _____ it 1:00 p.m.?   **A:** Yes, _____ .

4. **Q:** _____ you a college student?   **A:** Yes, _____ .

5. **Q:** _____ you in English classes?   **A:** No, _____ .

6. **Q:** _____ they school employees?   **A:** Yes, _____ .

7. **Q:** _____ he a teacher?   **A:** Yes, _____ .

8. **Q:** _____ your classes in the morning?   **A:** Yes, _____ .

2 Read each paragraph about Rita's classes. Complete the questions and answers. Use the full forms of *be* in short answers with *yes*. Use contractions in answers with *no*.

Rita is very busy this semester. She is in an English reading class on Monday morning. She is in English grammar and writing classes on Tuesday morning. Rita is in a math class after lunch on Tuesday and Thursday afternoons. Her math teacher is Mr. Ogun.

1. **Q:** ___*Is*___ Rita a student?   **A:** _*Yes, she is.*_____

2. **Q:** _____ the English grammar and writing classes on Tuesday morning?   **A:** _____

3. **Q:** _____ the English reading class on Tuesday afternoon?   **A:** _____

4. **Q:** _____ the math class on Tuesdays and Thursdays?   **A:** _____

5. **Q:** _____ the math class in the morning?   **A:** _____

6. **Q:** _____ Mr. Ogun the reading teacher?   **A:** _____

Rita is in a computer class on Monday and Wednesday afternoons. Andrea is a friend of Rita. They are in the same computer class. Their computer teacher is Ms. Wang.

7. **Q:** _____ Andrea and Rita in the same computer class?

   A: _____

8. **Q:** _____ the computer class on Monday and Wednesday mornings?

   A: _____

9. **Q:** _____ Rita and Andrea friends?

   A: _____

10. **Q:** _____ Ms. Wang their computer teacher?

    A: _____

3 Write questions and answers about each picture. Use the full forms of *be* in answers with *yes*. Use contractions in short answers with *no*.

1. nervous

   Q: *Is she nervous?*

   A: *Yes, she is.*

2. a teacher

   Q: _____

   A: _____

3. a student

   Q: _____

   A: _____

4. happy

   Q: _____

   A: _____

5. at a park

   Q: _____

   A: _____

6. students

   Q: _____

   A: _____

4 Write the questions. Then write answers about you. Use *am*, *is*, and *are*.

1. you / a student

   Q: *Are you a student?*   **A:** *Yes, I am.*

2. your English classes / interesting

   Q: _____   **A:** _____

3. your English class / difficult

   Q: _____   **A:** _____

4. you and your friends / in the same classes

   Q: _____   **A:** _____

Information Questions with *Be*

1 Match the questions with the correct answers.

1. **Q:** Where are you from? __*f*__   a. **A:** It's $1,500.

2. **Q:** Where is Tatiana? _____   b. **A:** He's 20 years old.

3. **Q:** How is your class? _____   c. **A:** She's in the library.

4. **Q:** Who's your adviser? _____   d. **A:** It's *The Woman Warrior*.

5. **Q:** When is your exam? _____   e. **A:** It's fun.

6. **Q:** How much is the tuition? _____   f. **A:** Ecuador.

7. **Q:** What's your favorite book? _____   g. **A:** Mrs. Young.

8. **Q:** How old is your roommate? _____   h. **A:** It's on Friday.

2 Complete the questions with the correct words from the box. Read the answers to help you.

Who	What	~~Where~~	When
How	How old	How much	How many

1. **Q:** _____*Where*_____ is your teacher?   **A:** He's in the classroom.

2. **Q** _____ are your classmates?   **A:** Tomás, Linh, Sofia, and Ahmet.

3. **Q:** _____ are your English classes?   **A:** Mondays and Wednesdays.

4. **Q:** _____ is your teacher's last name?   **A:** It's Nakamura.

5. **Q:** _____ is Mr. Nakamura?   **A:** He's 44 years old.

6. **Q:** _____ computers are in the lab?   **A:** Fifteen computers.

7. **Q:** _____ is tuition?   **A:** It's $2,000.

8. **Q:** _____ is school?   **A:** It's good.

3 Complete the phone conversation between Pedro and Mario. Use the full forms of *be* in questions. Use contractions in answers.

Mario: Hey, Pedro. It's Mario.

Pedro: Hi, Mario. How _*are*_ you?
$\qquad$ (1)

Mario: I'm fine. Where are you right now?

Pedro: Well, I _____ at work.
$\qquad$ (2)

Mario: Work? What _____ your job?
(3)

Pedro: I _____ a delivery boy for a restaurant.
(4)

Mario: What _____ the name of the restaurant?
(5)

Pedro: Milford Diner.

Mario: Where _____ it?
(6)

Pedro: On Fourth Street, next to the library.

Mario: Oh, right. What _____ your hours?
(7)

Pedro: From 7:00 to 11:00, four nights a week. Hey, Mario, when _____
(8)

our English exam?

Mario: On Friday.

Pedro: OK, Mario. We _____ really busy right now. See you tomorrow.
(9)

4 Write information questions about Samuel's class schedule. Then write the answers.

Plains Community College   *Fall Class Schedule*

Name: Samuel Chin
Student ID: 0054321   **Major:** Computer science

Course	Day	Time
Computer Programming I	T / TH	9–12
ESL Writing	M / W	1–3
Chemistry	M / W	9–11
Psychology	T / TH	1–3

1. What / his major

   Q: *What is his major?*   **A:** *His major is computer science.*

2. When / the writing course

   Q: _____   **A:** _____

3. What time / the chemistry course

   Q: _____   **A:** _____

4. Write your own question and answer.

   Q: _____   **A:** _____

Avoid Common Mistakes

1 Circle the mistakes.

1. (When your) class? <u>**Where is your**</u> class? <u>**Who is in your**</u> class?
   (a)   (b)   (c)

2. <u>**Are**</u> you a student? <u>**is**</u> she a student? <u>**Am**</u> I your teacher?
   (a)   (b)   (c)

3. <u>**How your teacher is**</u>? <u>**How are**</u> you? <u>**How much is**</u> that?
   (a)   (b)   (c)

4. <u>**Are you**</u> in the cafeteria? <u>**Are we**</u> on time for class? <u>**Is you**</u> and Bill in the library?
   (a)   (b)   (c)

5. When is your exam <u>**?**</u> Who is my teacher <u>**.**</u> Where is the classroom <u>**?**</u>
   (a)   (b)   (c)

6. **A:** Is your roommate nice? **B:** <u>**Yes, she is.**</u> **A:** Am I late? **B:** <u>**Yes, you are.**</u> **A:** Are your friends here?
                                    (a)   (b)

   B: <u>**Yes, they're.**</u>
          (c)

7. <u>**What's your**</u> name? <u>**When are his**</u> classes? <u>**How old your**</u> roommate?
   (a)   (b)   (c)

8. How old <u>**is she**</u>? <u>**What your instructor's name is**</u>? <u>**Where is**</u> the computer lab?
   (a)   (b)   (c)

2 Find and correct eight more mistakes in the interview with a director of a college English program.

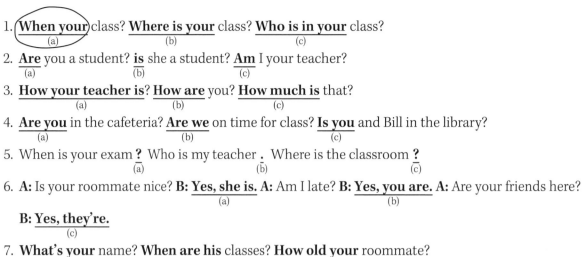

Palm College English Program: *An Interview with Professor Rawlings*

1. **Q:** How many students ~~is~~ *are* in the English program?   **A:** There are 1,000 students.

2. **Q:** Where they from?   **A:** They're from 30 different countries.

3. **Q:** Is they in other classes.   **A:** Yes, they're in science classes.

4. **Q:** are you an instructor for any large courses?   **A:** Yes, I'm. I teach English and biology.

5. **Q:** How long students are in your program?   **A:** For two years.

6. **Q:** Where the classes.   **A:** In Building D.

Self-Assessment

Circle the word or phrase that correctly completes each sentence.

1. _____ we free in the morning?

   a. Am   b. Are   c. Is

2. _____ the computer building?

   a. Where   b. Where are   c. Where is

3. **A:** Is your next class interesting? **B:** Yes, _____ .

   a. it is   b. it's   c. they are

4. _____ the computer lab and the library closed on weekends?

   a. Is   b. Are they   c. Are

5. _____ the academic writing center?

   a. Where is   b. Where   c. where is

6. _____ from Venezuela?

   a. Your friends   b. Are your friends   c. Is your friends

7. _____ the tuition at your school?

   a. Where is   b. How many is   c. How much is

8. **A:** Is your major math? **B:** _____

   a. No, it's not.   b. No, is not.   c. No, it no is.

9. **A:** Where are your classes? **B:** _____

   a. They are on Mondays and Wednesdays.   b. They're fun.   c. They are in Building C.

10. When is your next _____

   a. exam.   b. Exams.   c. exam?

11. _____ in your accounting class difficult?

   a. Is the quizzes   b. The quizzes are   c. Are the quizzes

12. **A:** Are the classrooms open at 6:00 a.m.? **B:** _____

   a. Yes, it is.   b. Yes, they're.   c. Yes, they are.

13. **A:** _____ is Mr. Perry? **B:** He's in class now.

   a. Where   b. When   c. How

14. **A:** _____ is your English instructor? **B:** She's very friendly.

   a. How old   b. What   c. How

15. **A:** _____ **B:** In Pakistan.

   a. Where are your parents?   b. Where your parents are?   c. How are your parents?

Count Nouns; *A/An*; *Have* and *Be*

Gadgets

Nouns; *A/An*

1 Complete the electronics store ad. Write *a* or *an* on each line.

MARTY'S ELECTRONICS BLACK FRIDAY SALE!
The Best Prices in Town!

1. __*a*__ digital camera   **$149⁹⁹**

2. _____ MP3 player   **$29⁹⁹**

3. _____ audio system   **$349⁹⁸**

4. _____ mobile phone   **$199⁹⁹**

5. _____ flat-screen TV   **$799⁹⁹**

6. _____ DVD player   **$59⁹⁹**

7. _____ computer   **$699⁹⁹**

8. _____ e-reader   **$119⁹⁹**

2 Write the plural forms of the nouns.

Regular Plural Nouns   **Irregular Plural Nouns**

1. city _____*cities*_____   9. child _____*children*_____

2. bus _____   10. foot _____

3. story_____   11. fish _____

4. company _____   12. sheep _____

5. schedule _____   13. man _____

6. library _____   14. woman _____

7. box _____   15. person _____

8. laptop _____   16. tooth _____

3 Complete the customer comments about different products from an online store. Write the plural nouns.

LiveLong Batteries:

1. Six __*batteries*__ (battery) are in a package.

2. Is the product safe for _____ (child)?

Guava WLX5 Laptop Computers:

3. Some _____ (man) and _____ (woman) will have problems using the small keyboard.

4. The computer parts are in too many _____ (box).

5. They're great _____ (laptop).

6. The different _____ (fish) on the screen saver are cute!

SongChirp Music Player:

7. The music _____ (library) are helpful. Good organization!

8. _____ (Person) are crazy about the new music player. It's great!

4 Circle the correct articles and nouns to complete the sentences.

1. (Michelle) / michelle is a /(an) engineer at Montell Computer Company.

2. Her company is in **California / california**.

3. The location is in **silicon valley / Silicon Valley**.

4. The company is the maker of **a / an** 3-D **Computer / computer**.

5. The name of the **machine / Machine** is **arion / Arion**.

6. **Antonio / antonio** is **a / an** software developer for the 3-D model.

7. He is happy with the **Product / product**. It has **a / an** large screen.

8. It's on sale now at **big electric / Big Electric** electronics store.

Be with *A/An* + Noun

1 Read the conversation between a customer and a sales clerk at an electronics store. Complete the sentences with *a* or *an*.

Customer: What's a good cell phone model?

Salesclerk: Here's the Max4. It's ___an___ excellent model. It's only $199.99.
(1)

Customer: It's _____ good price, but it isn't _____ good color.
(2) (3)

Salesclerk: Well, what about _____ Opal X-20 model? It's available in blue, green, red,
(4)

and pink.

Customer: _____ blue model is good. Is it _____ Internet-ready model?
(5) (6)

Salesclerk: It's _____ smartphone. You're always online, day or night. _____
(7) (8)

plastic case and _____ extra charger are part of the package.
(9)

Customer: Great!

2 Jessica tells her class about her friends' occupations. Use the words below to complete her sentences. Use *am* or *is* with *a* or *an* for singular nouns and *are* with no article for plural nouns.

Name	Occupation	Jessica:
1. Bill	chef	*Bill is a chef.*
2. Alex and Maria	architects	
3. Jane	electrician	
4. Tae-Woo	pharmacist	
5. Sue and Mark	instructors	
6. You	students	
7. Andrei and Bob	pilots	
8. Samir	artist	
9. I	part-time student	
10. My husband and I	salesclerks	

3 Write sentences to complete the review of the Z-150 camera. Use *be* with *a*, *an*, or no article.

Camera Review

The Z-150 camera is a new product (The Z-150 camera / new product) on the
(1)

market. It is from Grant Electronics. However, _____
(2)

(it / terrible camera)! _____ (It / bad buy) with a price
(3)

of $600.

_____ (Its models / ugly colors). They are pink, gold,
(4)

silver, and olive. Also, _____ (it / old model).
(5)

_____ (It / not / digital camera).
(6)

_____ (It / film camera) similar to the 1960s models!
(7)

Also, _____ (its flash / separate attachment).
(8)

It's so heavy!

The picture here is from the Z-150. _____
(9)

(It / blurry photo) of the beach. How

ugly! The camera's film is also very

expensive. According to GizmoNews,

_____
(10)

_____

(the Z-150 camera / awful product).

---

4 Write sentences about you and your classmates. Use *am* or *is* and *a* or *an* with the words below.

1. good student   _Alana is a good student._ _____

2. interesting person   _____

3. special teacher   _____

Now write true sentences about new gadgets.

4. expensive phone   _____

5. important gadget   _____

Have

1 Complete the sentences. Use *have* or *has*.

1. Mary _*has*_ three brothers.

2. Her brothers _____ laptops.

3. The computers _____ Internet access.

4. Her brother John _____ a new car.

5. The car _____ satellite radio.

6. Two of her brothers _____ a flat-screen TV.

7. The flat-screen TV _____ Internet.

8. Mary _____ an old TV.

9. It _____ a bad picture.

10. The brothers _____ a new TV for Mary.

2 Complete the sentences using *have*, *has*, *is*, *am*, or *are*.

| send | attach | save draft | forward | close |

From:	Liliana Gomez <lgomez85@cambridge.org>
To:	Rafael Gomez <rgomez83@cambridge.org>
Subject:	Help!

Hi Rafa,

I _____*have*_____ an old computer, so my Internet connection _____
        (1)   (2)
slow. I _____ not happy about that. Where _____ your old
        (3)   (4)
laptop? _____ it in our house? _____ it OK for me to use it?
         (5)   (6)
My roommates _____ a much faster computer. They _____
              (7)   (8)
really nice, and I _____ permission to use their computer sometimes. It
                    (9)
_____ a really fast Internet connection. My computer _____ so
 (10)   (11)
bad! I think you _____ the answer. Please call me.
                  (12)

Thanks,

Lil

3 Read the chart below from the Electronics Comparison website. Write sentences about each phone's features. Use *have* and *has* with *a* or *an*.

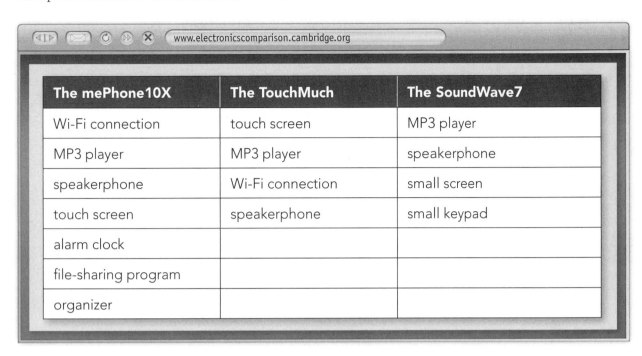

www.electronicscomparison.cambridge.org

The mePhone10X	The TouchMuch	The SoundWave7
Wi-Fi connection	touch screen	MP3 player
MP3 player	MP3 player	speakerphone
speakerphone	Wi-Fi connection	small screen
touch screen	speakerphone	small keypad
alarm clock		
file-sharing program		
organizer		

1. small keypad   *The SoundWave7 has a small keypad.*

2. alarm clock   _____

3. Wi-Fi connection   _____

4. MP3 player   _____

5. file-sharing program   _____

6. organizer   _____

7. speakerphone   _____

8. touch screen   _____

4 Write about yourself. What are some gadgets people you know have?

1. My friend *has a laptop* _____ .

2. I _____ .

3. The school _____ .

4. My classmates and I _____ .

5. My neighbors _____ .

6. The instructor _____ .

Avoid Common Mistakes

1 Circle the mistakes.

1. Melissa is **a nurse**. He is **an engineer**. You are (pilot).
   (a)   (b)   (c)

2. The cell phone **has** many features. It **have** a camera. Many cell phones **have** a camera.
   (a)   (b)   (c)

3. They **are** in an office. The office **is** new. The women **is** architects.
   (a)   (b)   (c)

4. The smart phone **have** Internet access. It **has** text messaging. It **has** a video recorder.
   (a)   (b)   (c)

5. The TV and DVD player **is** easy to use. They **are** on sale today. They **are** not expensive.
   (a)   (b)   (c)

6. The men **are** chefs. The products **is** helpful. The laptops **are** very small.
   (a)   (b)   (c)

7. Sue and Joe **is** students. My phone and laptop **are** here. The E-reader and MP3 player
   (a)   (b)

   are new.
   (c)

8. She is **an excellent doctor**. She is **kind person**. He is **a patient person**.
   (a)   (b)   (c)

2 Find and correct eight more mistakes in the review from *Car Magazine*.

Review: The Metra 98X

The new Metra 98X sport utility vehicle (SUV) is very popular. Families ~~is~~ *are*

happy with it. Children and parents is happy with the small TV in the back seat.

This SUV have many new features. It has a big gas tank – great for long trips.

It have eight seats. The seats is big and comfortable. The color and design is

very attractive. It has a great price at $25,000. Mrs. Franks is busy person. She is

architect. She have a Metra 98X. It is great for her work and her family.

Self-Assessment

Circle the word or phrase that correctly completes each sentence.

1. The battery life is eight _____ .

   a. hour   b. houres   c. hours

2. The DVD player is _____ .

   a. a old model   b. an old model   c. old model

3. Roberto and Maria are in _____ .

   a. Bangkok, Thailand   b. bangkok, thailand   c. Bangkok, thailand

4. This is _____ for me.

   a. good computer   b. a good computer   c. good computers

5. Ana is _____ .

   a. nice teacher   b. teacher   c. a nice teacher

6. The laptop and printer _____ on sale.

   a. are   b. is   c. have

7. I _____ a new cell phone.

   a. has   b. am   c. have

8. Katia and Ryan are _____ .

   a. a good engineers   b. a good engineer   c. good engineers

9. Susan has _____ next week.

   a. a quiz   b. quiz   c. a quizzes

10. Many _____ have cell phones today.

    a. childrens   b. children   c. childs

11. We _____ a computer lab at school.

    a. has   b. have   c. are

12. A picture of my son _____ on my new phone.

    a. is   b. have   c. has

13. The games on my new computer _____ .

    a. are fun   b. have fun   c. has fun

14. The people in my office _____ very friendly.

    a. is   b. have   c. are

15. _____ has great gadgets on sale today.

    a. winston electronics   b. Winston Electronics   c. Winston electronics

Demonstratives and Possessives
The Workplace

Demonstratives (*This, That, These, Those*)

1 Look at the pictures. Complete the sentences. Use *This, That, These,* or *Those.*

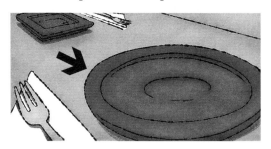

1. ___*This*___ plate is round.

2. _____ glass is full.

3. _____ forks are on the napkin.

4. _____ napkin is black.

5. _____ spoons are clean.

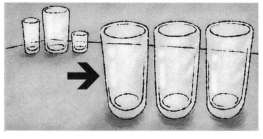

6. _____ cups are the same size.

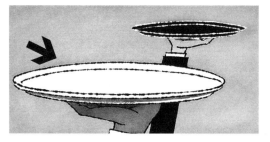

7. _____ tray is white.

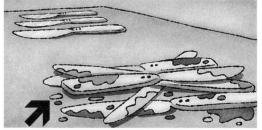

8. _____ knives are dirty.

2 Complete the conversation between Tara and the restaurant manager. Use *this*, *that*, *these*, or *those*.

Manager: Is today your first day?

Tara: Yes, it is.

Manager: OK. Well, __*these*__ plates here go on _____ table over there. _____
　　　　　　　　　(1)　　　　　　　　　　　　　　　　(2)　　　　　　　　　　　　　　(3)

napkins over there are for _____ tables right here. _____ cups over
　　　　　　　　　　　　　　　　(4)　　　　　　　　　　　　　　　(5)

there are for _____ table there.
　　　　　　　(6)

Tara: What about _____ spoons over there? And _____ tray here?
　　　　　　　　　　　　　(7)　　　　　　　　　　　　　　　(8)

Manager: The tray is for _____ table here. The spoons are for _____ table here, too.
　　　　　　　　　　　　　(9)　　　　　　　　　　　　　　　　　　　(10)

3 A supervisor is giving a tour to new employees at the Price Company. Read the sentences, and circle the correct demonstrative.

Welcome to the Price Company! (**This**)/**These** office is big, so here's a quick tour.
　　　　　　　　　　　　　　　　(1)

First, **this**/**that** is the conference room over there. It's for all our large meetings. Next,
　　　　　(2)

those/**that** area is the cafeteria. **That**/**This** is the hot food over there, and **that**/**this**
　　(3)　　　　　　　　　　　　　　(4)　　　　　　　　　　　　　　　　　　　(5)

is the drink area right here. Oh look, **that**/**these** man is Mr. Smith. He's the manager
　　　　　　　　　　　　　　　　(6)

of accounting. **That**/**This** is his office over there. And **that**/**those** people are his team
　　　　　　　(7)　　　　　　　　　　　　　　　　　　(8)

members in the next room. **That**/**This** room, here, is the copy center, and **these**/**that** are
　　　　　　　　　　　　　(9)　　　　　　　　　　　　　　　　　　　(10)

the copy machines. Well, that's it for the tour today. I hope **this**/**those** is helpful.
　　　　　　　　　　　　　　　　　　　　　　　　　　　　(11)

4 Tom is at a new job. Complete Tom's questions about the office. Use a form of *be* and *this*, *that*, *these*, or *those*. Use the words in parentheses to help you. Then complete the answers with *It's*, *She's*, *He's*, or *They're*.

1. What __*is this*__ room? (near)

　__*It's*__ the conference room.

2. Who _____ people in it? (not near)

　_____ the new employees.

3. Who _____ man? (not near)

　_____ the new sales manager on your team.

4. Where _____ customer folders? (not near)

　_____ over there on that desk.

5. What _____ box? (near)

　_____ a new printer.

6. What _____ boxes on the cabinet? (near)

_____ office supplies for your sales team.

7. Who _____ woman? (near)

_____ the president of the company.

Possessives and *Whose*

1 Complete the chart with the correct possessives.

Subject	Possessive	Subject	Possessive
I	1. *my*	it	5.
you	2.	we	6.
he	3.	they	7.
she	4.	who	8.

2 Complete the comments from different people about their office. Use *my, your, his, her, our, its,* or *their*.

1. **Sue and Keiko** work in Hong Kong. _Their_ company is new.

2. **Juliana** is an excellent boss. _____ employees are very happy.

3. **Mark** is an IT manager. _____ team is very big.

4. **I** am very organized. _____ desk is always neat.

5. **The conference room** is comfortable. _____ chairs are leather.

6. **We** have a great sales team. _____ team has 10 employees.

7. **The printer** has a problem. _____ paper drawer is empty.

8. **You** are a wonderful employee. _____ work is always careful.

9. **She** is my co-worker. _____ office is always organized.

10. **I** have a lot of work experience. _____ résumé is really great.

3 Complete the paragraph. Use possessive nouns.

My friend Erika has a great job. She is the _*president's*_ (president) assistant. Her

_____ (company) offices are wonderful. They are on the 56th floor of the
(2)

_____ (city) tallest building. The _____ (employees) offices
(3)   (4)

all have windows. _____ (Erika) office also has a big video screen for
                          (5)

meetings. The _____ (managers) schedules are on the network calendar.
                      (6)

The _____ (department) network is good, so the calendar is always
            (7)

organized. With this system, the _____ (assistant) job is always easy. Erika
                                            (8)

is very happy at her job.

4 Read the information below. Write information questions and answers with *Whose* and
Who's with possessive nouns and possessive pronouns. Use a form of *be* for
the answers.

Wilson Hotel Employee Data		
Sharon Jones	**Edward Garcia**	**Lili Kang**
Phone: 555-4431	Phone: 555-4426	Phone: 555-4439
Office: Room AF231	Office: Room AF236	Office: Room AF200
Employee ID: 54021	Employee ID: 24026	Employee ID: 57789
Job title: Hotel Receptionist	Job title: Hotel Manager	Job title: Hotel Chef
Salary: $35,000 / year	Salary: $75,000 / year	Salary: $45,000 / year
Manager: Jim Rock	Manager: Beverly Eung	Manager: Teresa Romano

1. Who / Sharon / manager

   Who's Sharon's manager?   *Her manager is Jim Rock.*

2. Whose / job title / hotel manager

   Whose job title is hotel manager?   *Edward's job title is hotel manager.*

3. Who / Edward / manager

   _____   _____

4. Whose / office / Room AF236

   _____   _____

5. Whose / employee ID / 57789

   _____   _____

6. Who / Lili / manager

   _____   _____

7. Whose / salary / $35,000

   _____   _____

Avoid Common Mistakes

1 Circle the mistakes.

1. My **brother's** name is Irish. **His** wife's name is French. His (**childrens**) names

‾‾(a)‾‾   ‾‾(b)‾‾   ‾‾(c)‾‾

are English.

2. **This** is a bad cabinet. **It's** doors are broken. **It's** under my desk.

‾‾(a)‾‾   ‾‾(b)‾‾   ‾‾(c)‾‾

3. **This** is her desk. These are **hers** files. This is **her** mail.

‾‾(a)‾‾   ‾‾(b)‾‾   ‾‾(c)‾‾

4. **This** photos are beautiful. **Those** are nice, too. But **these** are the best.

‾‾(a)‾‾   ‾‾(b)‾‾   ‾‾(c)‾‾

5. That's the **man** work ID number. **His** ID number is short. **It's** easy to remember.

‾‾(a)‾‾   ‾‾(b)‾‾   ‾‾(c)‾‾

6. **These** are the employees. **Those** are their desks. **These** is their company.

‾‾(a)‾‾   ‾‾(b)‾‾   ‾‾(c)‾‾

7. **A:** How much is **that** webcam? **B: Its** $25. **A: That's** a great price.

‾‾(a)‾‾   ‾‾(b)‾‾   ‾‾(c)‾‾

8. Those are **our** reports. **These** is our meeting room. These are **their** supplies.

‾‾(a)‾‾   ‾‾(b)‾‾   ‾‾(c)‾‾

2 Find and correct eight more mistakes in the e-mail to Chris from his boss.

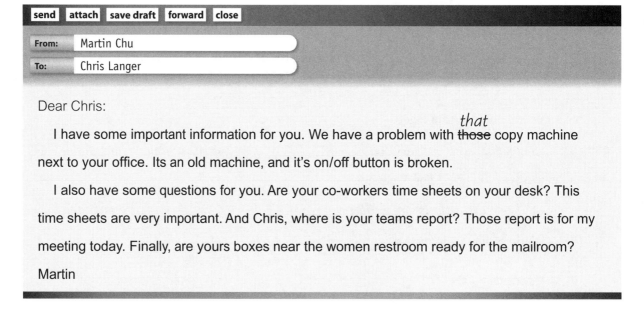

send   attach   save draft   forward   close

From: Martin Chu

To: Chris Langer

Dear Chris:

    I have some important information for you. We have a problem with ~~those~~ *that* copy machine

next to your office. Its an old machine, and it's on/off button is broken.

    I also have some questions for you. Are your co-workers time sheets on your desk? This

time sheets are very important. And Chris, where is your teams report? Those report is for my

meeting today. Finally, are yours boxes near the women restroom ready for the mailroom?

Martin

Self-Assessment

Circle the word or phrase that correctly completes each sentence.

1. The _____ are in the conference room.

   a. teams charts   b. team's charts   c. team charts'

2. _____ are on my desk.

   a. Those reports   b. That reports   c. These report

3. My boss has a report about _____ .

   a. these employee   b. that employee   c. this employees

4. The business is successful. _____ workers are very happy there.

   a. Her   b. His   c. Its

5. Those are _____ in the picture.

   a. my brother's children   b. my brothers children   c. my brothers children's

6. The calculator is old. Some of _____ are broken.

   a. it's keys   b. it keys   c. its keys

7. _____ are the office supplies for the receptionist.

   a. That   b. These   c. This

8. All the managers have a meeting today. Is the _____ on this floor?

   a. managers' meeting   b. manager's meeting   c. managers meeting

9. She is at a big computer company. _____ job title is computer programmer.

   a. Her   b. Its   c. Hers

10. The _____ is down this hallway.

    a. womens restroom   b. women restroom   c. women's restroom

11. The Posh Company is good to its employees. _____ a great place to work.

    a. Its   b. It's   c. It

12. All the _____ are empty today. They all have the day off.

    a. supervisors offices   b. supervisor offices'   c. supervisors' offices

13. _____ cabinet over there is not closed. Please close it.

    a. That   b. This   c. Those

14. The reports are in _____ folders here.

    a. this   b. these   c. those

15. These photos are of _____ trip to Florida.

    a. my bosses   b. my boss   c. my boss's

Descriptive Adjectives

Skills and Qualities for Success

Adjectives

1 Look at the online job descriptions. Rewrite the sentences. Use the adjectives in parentheses to describe the nouns in bold. Change the article when necessary.

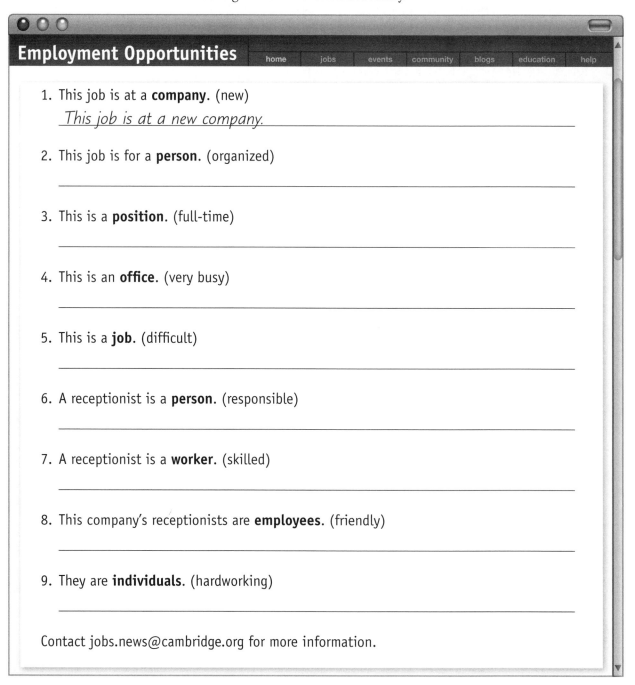

Employment Opportunities   home   jobs   events   community   blogs   education   help

1. This job is at a **company**. (new)
   This job is at a new company.

2. This job is for a **person**. (organized)

3. This is a **position**. (full-time)

4. This is an **office**. (very busy)

5. This is a **job**. (difficult)

6. A receptionist is a **person**. (responsible)

7. A receptionist is a **worker**. (skilled)

8. This company's receptionists are **employees**. (friendly)

9. They are **individuals**. (hardworking)

Contact jobs.news@cambridge.org for more information.

2 Look at the picture. Complete the sentences about the office and the people in it. Use *be* + the adjectives in the box.

Ken Malik Sally Isabella

asleep	disorganized	new	sad
busy	happy	old	~~very small~~

1. The call center _is very small_ .

2. The call center has a lot of papers and boxes. It _____ .

3. The call center has many employees. It _____ .

4. Sally and Isabella _____ .

5. Ken _____ .

6. Ken's and Malik's computers _____ .

7. Sally's and Isabella's computers _____ .

8. Malik _____ .

3 Write sentences about the people below. Use the adjectives in the box or your own ideas. Use adjective + noun or *be* + adjective.

ambitious	~~fast~~	good	interesting	organized
excellent	friendly	hardworking	kind	smart

1. learner _I am a fast learner._

2. students _____

3. worker _____

4. teachers _____

5. employee _____

6. boss _____

4 Read John's description of the people in his office. Complete the sentences with the correct nationality.

The people at my job are from many different places. Ismael is our manager. He is from Lima, **Peru**. He is _Peruvian_ . Jin-Sun is our accountant. She is from Seoul in **South** (1)

Korea. She is _____ . We have three sales representatives. Tam is from Hanoi (2)

in **Vietnam**. He is _____ . Emily is from London in **Great Britain**. She is (3)

_____ . Doria is from Athens in **Greece**. She is _____ . (4) (5)

Our receptionist is Janet. She is from New York City in the **United States**. She is

_____ . My good friend, Silvio, is the computer technician. He is from São (6)

Paolo in **Brazil**. He is _____ . I am the computer programmer. I am from (7)

Shanghai, **China**. I am the only _____ person in the office. Our interns (8)

are Sandra and Alex. Sandra is from **Canada**, and she is the only _____ in (9)

the office. Alex is from the **Philippines**. He is our first _____ intern at the (10)

company. The president of the company is Feride. She is from Istanbul, **Turkey**. She is

_____ . Her assistant, Patrick, is from Amsterdam in the **Netherlands**. He is (11)

the only _____ person in our office. We have a lot of fun in the office. (12)

Questions with *What . . . like?* and *How* + Adjective

1 Jeff is at his company's São Paolo office. Match the questions and answers about Jeff's experience.

1. **Q:** What's São Paolo like? _d_
2. **Q:** How friendly are the employees? ____
3. **Q:** What are the offices like? ____
4. **Q:** How hot is it there? ____
5. **Q:** What's your hotel room like? ____
6. **Q:** What's the food like? ____
7. **Q:** How high are prices there? ____

a. **A:** It's very big.
b. **A:** It's a little warm and rainy.
c. **A:** It's delicious.
d. **A:** It's very busy and crowded.
e. **A:** Things are cheap.
f. **A:** They're very comfortable.
g. **A:** They're very friendly.

2 A Write questions about Jeff's company. Use *How + be.*

1. tall / their building   *How tall is their building?*

2. nice / the co-workers   _____

3. large / the company   _____

4. difficult / the work   _____

5. big / the offices   _____

B Now write questions about Jeff's company with *What . . . like?*

1. their building   *What's their building like?*

2. the co-workers   _____

3. the company   _____

4. the work   _____

5. the offices   _____

3 Read the paragraphs about Marta's job. Write the questions and answers.

Marta is hardworking and ambitious. She is 24 years old. Her job is at a one-year-old social networking website called MySpot. The job is fun and interesting. Marta's powerful new computer is perfect for her work.

1. What . . . like / Marta   **Q:** *What is Marta like?*

    A: *She's hardworking and ambitious.*

2. How / old / Marta   **Q:** _____

    A: _____

3. What . . . like / Marta's new computer   **Q:** _____

    A: _____

Marta's boss, Ms. Stewart, is kind and flexible. Her co-workers are young and energetic. She is very happy with her job. It is not difficult for her. It is easy and relaxing. However, Marta's hours at work are very long, from 7 a.m. to 6 p.m. Her dinner is always late, after 9 p.m.

4. What . . . like / her boss   **Q:** _____

    A: _____

5. How / difficult / her job   **Q:** _____

    A: _____

6. How / long / her hours   **Q:** _____

    A: _____

Avoid Common Mistakes

1 Circle the mistakes.

1. My friend is **a** good person, ~~**a**~~ excellent student, and **a** hard worker.

(a)   (b)   (c)

2. Her **small office** is dark. It has **old desks** and **windows dirty**.

(a)   (b)   (c)

3. My city has **friendly people**, **beautifuls parks**, and **nice weather**.

(a)   (b)   (c)

4. Paulo is **American**. His mother is **Argentinean**. His father is **brazilian**.

(a)   (b)   (c)

5. My apartment building is **crowded**. It has a lot of **noisy children**, and the **music loud**.

(a)   (b)   (c)

6. John is a **swedish** accountant. His company **is big**. His boss is **French**.

(a)   (b)   (c)

7. I am not excited about my **new job**. It has **longs hours** and a **low salary**.

(a)   (b)   (c)

8. The website has **a interesting blog**, **a useful link** to résumés, and **an extra page**

(a)   (b)   (c)

for photos.

2 Find and correct eight more mistakes on the employer profile below.

> ## Goodtime Travel–*Employer Profile*
>
> We are ~~a~~ *an* American travel agency on the border of the United States and Mexico. We have
>
> Mexicans customers and american customers. We have an special offer right now on our tour
>
> to Mexico City. We also have an exciting tour to guatemalan places of interest. We have 20
>
> employees friendly. We also have an attractive website with photos beautiful. Our company
>
> has very youngs employees. Our office comfortable. Goodtime Travel is a good workplace.

Self-Assessment

Circle the word or phrase that correctly completes each sentence.

1. I have _____ in my company.

   a. an quiet office   b. an office quiet   c. a quiet office

2. The networking site has links to _____ .

   a. interesting businesses   b. businesses interesting   c. interestings businesses

3. The software company has _____ customers.

   a. chinese and japanese   b. China and Japan   c. Chinese and Japanese

4. Anna is ____ manager.

   a. ambitious   b. an ambitious   c. a ambitious

5. Working in a new country is ____ for my career.

   a. a exciting goal   b. a goal exciting   c. an exciting goal

6. The ____ has an office in New York.

   a. korean company   b. Korean company   c. company korean

7. The social networking website has ____ on its home page.

   a. a link broken   b. an broken link   c. a broken link

8. **A:** How's ____? **B:** It's sunny and warm.

   a. the weather   b. the weather like   c. weather

9. Maria and Rita are ____ . They are at work over 50 hours a week.

   a. hardworking professionals   b. a professionals hardworking   c. hardworkings professionals

10. With a social networking site, you have a community of ____ online.

    a. friends good   b. good friends   c. friend good

11. ____ like?

    a. What's your job new   b. What your new job   c. What's your new job

12. David is ____ soccer player. He is on a Los Angeles team.

    a. an british   b. a British   c. an British

13. The ____ is 30 years old.

    a. unemployed accountant   b. accountant unemployed   c. accountants unemployed

14. Pedro and Irina are ____ . They are in a dance company in New York.

    a. brazilian dancers   b. Brazilian dancers   c. Brazil Dancers

15. Maria is ____ .

    a. a excellent employee   b. an excellent employee   c. an employee excellent

Prepositions

Around the House

Prepositions of Place: Things at Home and in the Neighborhood

1 Look at the picture. Circle the correct prepositions of place.

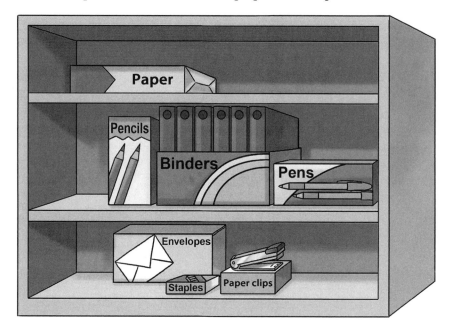

1. All the office supplies are **in** / **on** the cabinet.

2. The paper for the printer is **on** / **under** the top shelf.

3. Pens and pencils are on the shelf **under** / **behind** the paper.

4. Binders are **between** / **above** the pencils and pens.

5. The shelf with the paper is **next to** / **above** the shelf with the binders.

6. The staples are **in front of** / **behind** the envelopes.

7. The paper clips are **between** / **next to** the staples.

8. The envelopes are **in front of** / **behind** the staples.

9. The stapler is **under** / **on top of** the paper clips.

2 Look at the picture. Write sentences about the items in the refrigerator. Use the prepositions in the box.

above	between	~~next to~~	on top of
behind	in front of	next to	under

1. the milk / the water   *The milk is next to the water.* _____

2. the apples / the oranges _____

3. the eggs / the milk _____

4. the milk / the eggs _____

5. the fish / the bread _____

6. the fish / the carrots _____

7. the carrots / the corn and the onions _____

8. the vegetables / the fish _____

3 Complete the sentences about the places in Smithtown. Use the picture and the prepositions in the box. You can use prepositions more than once.

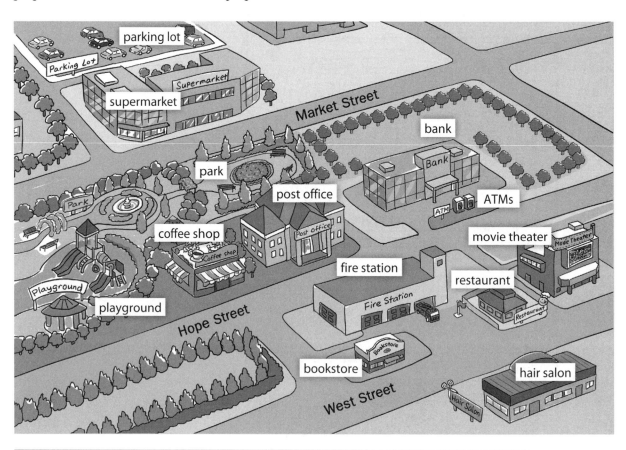

across from	behind	between	in front of	inside	next to	on

The supermarket is _on_ Market Street. A park is _____ the supermarket.
(1)   (2)

A playground is _____ the park. A parking lot is _____
(3)   (4)

the supermarket. _____ the playground is a coffee shop. A post office
(5)

is _____ the coffee shop and a bank on Hope Street. Two ATMs are
(6)

_____ the bank. A fire station is _____ the post office.
(7)   (8)

_____ the fire station is a bookstore. _____ West Street, a movie
(9)   (10)

theater is _____ the restaurant. A hair salon is _____ the fire
(11)   (12)

station.

Prepositions of Place: Locations and Other Uses

1 Complete the information about the places below with *in*, *on*, or *at*.

1. __on__ Second Street
2. _____ Chicago
3. _____ 301 Church Avenue
4. _____ California
5. _____ the tenth floor

6. _____ downtown Los Angeles
7. _____ Mexico
8. _____ 35 Broadway
9. _____ Summit Avenue
10. _____ Japan

2 Complete the paragraph about Brian and his family using *in*, *on*, or *at*.

Brian is _at_ work. He's _____ a meeting. His office is
₍₁₎ _____ (2)
_____ 17 Thomas Avenue _____ the sixteenth floor.
₍₃₎ _____ (4)
His home is _____ Dallas, Texas. Right now, his wife is
₍₅₎
_____ a clinic. She is a nurse _____ the third floor
₍₆₎ _____ (7)
of a Dallas health clinic. Their children are students. Their

son is a senior _____ college _____ the University of
₍₈₎ _____ (9)
Texas. Their daughter is _____ high school. Right now,
₍₁₀₎
both of the children are _____ school and _____
₍₁₁₎ _____ (12)
class. The only person _____ home is Brian's mother.
₍₁₃₎
She is _____ the second floor of the house. She is always
₍₁₄₎
_____ home.
₍₁₅₎

Brian and his family

3 Write answers to the questions. Use the information in parentheses with *in*, *on*, or *at*.

1. **Q:** What city is your home in? **A:** *My home is in San Diego.* (San Diego)
2. **Q:** What street is the school on? **A:** _____ (Park Avenue)
3. **Q:** Where are you now? **A:** _____ (work)
4. **Q:** Where is your job? **A:** _____ (1718 Sixth Street)
5. **Q:** Where are your friends? **A:** _____ (campus)
6. **Q:** Where is your brother? **A:** _____ (the post office)
7. **Q:** Where are your parents? **A:** _____ (the bank)
8. **Q:** What floor is your office on? **A:** _____ (the third floor)

4 Write sentences that are true for you. Use *in*, *on*, or *at*.

1. My home / street   *My home is on Monroe Street.*

2. My home / address   _____

3. I live / town or city   _____

4. I live / state or province _____

5. My school / street   _____

6. My school / address   _____

7. My English classroom / floor _____

Prepositions of Time

1 Write *in*, *on*, or *at* before each time expression.

1. __on__ Tuesday   7. _____ May 15, 2013

2. _____ the summer   8. _____ Friday

3. _____ six o'clock   9. _____ 2:15 p.m.

4. _____ Monday   10. _____ the winter

5. _____ June   11. _____ September 16

6. _____ the morning   12. _____ the afternoon

2 Complete the conversations with *in*, *on*, *at*, or *between*.

1. **A:** We have a birthday party for our cousin __on__ Saturday _____ 2:00 _____ the

(1)   (2)   (3)
   afternoon.

   B: No, it's _____ 3:00 _____ Sunday. Check the invitation.

(4)   (5)

2. **A:** Let's have lunch _____ the fall.

(6)

   B: OK. How about _____ a Friday _____ October?

(7)   (8)

   A: That's fine. Let's do it near your office _____ 12:30 and 2:00. OK?

(9)

3. **A:** I have a meeting _____ Monday _____ 1:00 p.m.

(10)   (11)

   B: I have a meeting, too. It begins _____ 2:00 p.m. and ends _____ 5:00 and 5:30.

(12)   (13)

   A: OK. Let's have dinner after that, _____ 7:00 _____ the evening.

(14)   (15)

3 A Write questions and short answers about the cruise schedule. Use the information below.

3-DAY PACIFIC COAST CRUISE SCHEDULE

MONDAY JUNE 22

5:00 P.M.	DEPARTURE FROM LOS ANGELES
8:00 P.M. – 10:00 P.M.	WELCOME DINNER

TUESDAY JUNE 23 (CONTINUED)

6:00 P.M. – 8:00 P.M.	DINNER
8:00 P.M. – 11:00 P.M.	DANCING

TUESDAY JUNE 23

6:00 A.M. – 10:00 A.M.	BREAKFAST
8:00 A.M.	YOGA CLASS
10:00 A.M.	SNACKS AND DRINKS
12:00 P.M. TO 2:00 P.M.	LUNCH
2:00 P.M.	ARRIVAL IN CABO SAN LUCAS, MEXICO
2:30 P.M. – 5:30 P.M.	SHOPPING IN CABO SAN LUCAS

WEDNESDAY JUNE 24

6:00 A.M. – 10:00 A.M.	BREAKFAST
8:00 A.M.	GROUP EXERCISE
10:00 A.M.	ARRIVAL IN SAN DIEGO
10:30 A.M.–3:30 P.M.	TOUR OF SAN DIEGO AND SHOPPING
6:00 P.M.	ARRIVAL IN LOS ANGELES
	– END OF CRUISE

1. first day of the cruise / when

   Q: _When is the first day of the cruise?_   **A:** _On Monday._

2. yoga class / what day

   Q: _____   **A:** _____

3. yoga class / what time of day

   Q: _____   **A:** _____

4. snacks and drinks / when

   Q: _____   **A:** _____

5. dancing / what day

   Q: _____   **A:** _____

6. dancing / what time

   Q: _____   **A:** _____

7. group exercise / what day

   Q: _____   **A:** _____

8. last day of the cruise / when

   Q: _____   **A:** _____

B Write three more questions and answers about the cruise schedule.

1. **Q:** When _is the welcome dinner?_   **A:** _On Monday._

2. **Q:** What day _____   **A:** _____

3. **Q:** What time _____   **A:** _____

4. **Q:** When _____   **A:** _____

Avoid Common Mistakes

1 Circle the mistakes.

1. My class is **at** 6 o'clock (**in**) Thursdays **in** the summer.
   (a)   (b)   (c)

2. Mary's home is **in** Atlanta, Georgia. She lives in an apartment **on** Park Street **in** second floor.
   (a)   (b)   (c)

3. The meeting is **in** 9:00 a.m. It's in the Lee Building **on** Fourth Street. It's **at** 354 Fourth Street.
   (a)   (b)   (c)

4. The people **in** my apartment building have a big party **on** April. It's **on** Hill Street.
   (a)   (b)   (c)

5. Jose is **in** Texas. His family is **in** Miami **on** 16 Paez Avenue.
   (a)   (b)   (c)

6. The salsa concert is **on** June 10. It is **on** 8:00 p.m. **on** Alvarado Street.
   (a)   (b)   (c)

7. I have a train ticket to Orlando **in** Florida. The train is **on** Track 5. The first train is **on** 4:00 a.m.
   (a)   (b)   (c)

8. Sue's birthday is **on** March 26. My birthday is **on** March, too. It's **on** St. Patrick's Day.
   (a)   (b)   (c)

2 Find and correct eight more mistakes in this student orientation announcement.

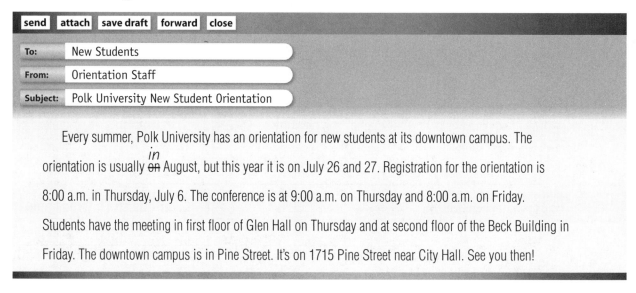

| send | attach | save draft | forward | close |

To: New Students

From: Orientation Staff

Subject: Polk University New Student Orientation

Every summer, Polk University has an orientation for new students at its downtown campus. The
orientation is usually ~~on~~ *in* August, but this year it is on July 26 and 27. Registration for the orientation is
8:00 a.m. in Thursday, July 6. The conference is at 9:00 a.m. on Thursday and 8:00 a.m. on Friday.
Students have the meeting in first floor of Glen Hall on Thursday and at second floor of the Beck Building in
Friday. The downtown campus is in Pine Street. It's on 1715 Pine Street near City Hall. See you then!

Self-Assessment

Circle the word or phrase that correctly completes each sentence.

1. Can you call me _____ tonight?

   a. on 7:30   b. in 7:30   c. at 7:30

2. My regular meetings are _____ the mornings.

   a. in   b. at   c. on

3. Registration is _____ 10:00 a.m. and 3:00 p.m.

    a. in   b. between   c. on

4. The parking lot is _____ the supermarket.

    a. in front   b. in front of   c. front of

5. The supermarket is _____ the parking lot.

    a. behind   b. behind of   c. behind to

6. My vacation is _____ .

    a. May   b. at May   c. in May

7. My workday begins every day _____ .

    a. at 8:00 a.m.   b. on 8:00 a.m.   c. 8:00 a.m.

8. Ivan's flight from Russia is _____ October 3.

    a. at   b. on   c. in

9. My mother's home is _____ .

    a. on Canada   b. in Canada   c. Canada

10. My boss's office is _____ the tenth floor.

    a. at   b. in   c. on

11. David's printer is _____ his desk.

    a. between   b. above   c. on top

12. The bank is _____ the coffee shop.

    a. next to   b. near at   c. across to

13. **A:** Where's Truc? **B:** She's _____ .

    a. at school   b. in work   c. on a meeting

14. **A:** When is Independence Day in the United States? **B:** It's _____ .

    a. on July   b. at July   c. in July.

15. Kim's home is _____ .

    a. at Bell Road   b. at 1613 Bell Road   c. at New York

There Is / There Are

1 Complete the paragraph below about the trains in a country Marc knows well. Circle the correct words.

The train system in the country is very modern and useful. **There's /(There are)**
                                                                          (1)

over 5,000 miles of train tracks and about 500 train cars. **There's / There are** 46 different
                                                                            (2)

train routes. **There's / There are** an exact schedule for each route. The trains are
              (3)

always on time. **There's / There are** train stations in all the big cities and towns.
                (4)

There isn't / There aren't any train service in some rural[1] areas, but **there's / there are**
        (5)   (6)

buses from these areas to nearby train stations. **There isn't / There aren't** any ticket
                                                          (7)

windows in many stations. **There's / There are** only ticket machines. Train security is
                          (8)

excellent, and **there isn't / there aren't** any problems with crime on the trains.
                        (9)

[1]**rural:** not in cities; the country

2 A Read the advertisement for a family entertainment park. Write sentences with *There's,
There are, There isn't / There's no,* and *There aren't / There are no.*

1. fishing   *There's fishing.*

2. a zoo   _____

3. an outdoor pool   _____

4. a restaurant   _____

5. water slides   _____

6. meeting rooms   _____

7. race cars   _____

8. a lake   _____

9. picnic areas   _____

O'HARA'S FUN PARK

We have:
- fishing
- paddle boats
- an outdoor pool
- water slides
- race cars
- a lake

B Write sentences about your town. Use *There is*, *There are*, *There isn't*, and *There aren't* and *some* or *any*. Use the words in the box or your own ideas.

bike lanes	a gym	a mall	a park	public buses
~~department stores~~	a lake	a movie theater	a pool	a train station

1. *There are some department stores in my town.* _____

2. _____

3. _____

4. _____

3 Read the conversation between two friends. Complete the sentences. Use *There's*, *There are*, *It's*, and *They're*.

Sonia: Let's eat at a restaurant tonight, Greg.

Greg: Great! _*There's*_ a popular restaurant near my job. _____
             (1)   (2)
a traditional Japanese restaurant.

Sonia: OK. That's a possibility. Any other ideas?

Greg: Yeah, _____ a small restaurant near your place. _____
                  (3)   (4)
new and has American food.

Sonia: How is the service?

Greg: _____ one hostess and many waiters and waitresses, and
              (5)
_____ very friendly. Also, the wait isn't long at all!
              (6)

Sonia: How is the food selection?

Greg: The food is delicious, and _____ many choices on the menu.
                                          (7)
_____ all healthy choices.
              (8)

Sonia: Great. _____ a café near that restaurant. _____ open late
                  (9)   (10)
and has live music. We can go there after dinner.

Greg: Sounds like fun. But remember, I have work tomorrow morning.

4 Complete the sentences with *There is*, *There are*, *There isn't*, and *There aren't*. Add more information. Use *It's* or *They're* and your own ideas.

1. ___There is___ a café in my neighborhood.   ___It's very popular._____

2. _____ parks in my neighborhood.   _____

3. _____ a museum downtown.   _____

4. _____ beach near here.   _____

5. _____ historic buildings in my town.   _____

6. _____ famous restaurants here.   _____

7. _____ a good movie theater near here.   _____

8. _____ big bookstores downtown.   _____

Yes / No Questions with *There Is* / *There Are*

1 The Garcia family's new home is in a new neighborhood. Complete the questions with *Is there / Are there* and write short answers with *there is* (*not*) or *there are* (*not*).

1. **Q:** ___Are there___ any big parks near the neighborhood?   **A:** Yes, ___there are___ .

2. **Q:** _____ a good school for children?   **A:** Yes, _____ .

3. **Q:** _____ a nice gym in the area?   **A:** No, _____ .

4. **Q:** _____ any friendly neighbors?   **A:** Yes, _____ .

5. **Q:** _____ a shopping mall in the area?   **A:** No, _____ .

6. **Q:** _____ a supermarket in the neighborhood?   **A:** Yes, _____ .

7. **Q:** _____ any other children in the neighborhood?   **A:** No, _____ .

8. **Q:** _____ any people from different cultures?   **A:** Yes, _____ .

9. **Q:** _____ a library nearby?   **A:** No, _____ .

10. **Q:** _____ a bank in the area?   **A:** Yes, _____ .

2 Read the review about places to visit in Washington, D.C. Then answer the questions with *there is*, *there are*, *there isn't*, and *there aren't*. Give short or long responses.

Washington, D.C., is an interesting and historic city. It's the capital of the United States. There are many museums, such as the National Air and Space Museum, the National Gallery of Art, and the National Postal Museum. There are over 70 museums in the Washington area. There are also historic buildings, like Ford's Theatre. There are no tall buildings. There's the National Zoo on Connecticut Avenue. It's the home of two giant pandas.

1. **Q:** Are there any museums in Washington, D.C.?   **A:** *Yes, there are over 70 museums.*

2. **Q:** Are there any historic buildings in Washington, D.C.?   **A:** _____

3. **Q:** Is there a zoo?   **A:** _____

4. **Q:** Are there any tall buildings?   **A:** _____

The White House is another popular attraction in Washington. It's the home of the president of the United States. There's the U.S. Capitol, the Washington Monument, the Lincoln Memorial, and the Library of Congress. They're all well-known places to visit. Washington, D.C., is a great place to learn about the history of the United States.

5. **Q:** Are there any monuments in Washington, D.C.?   **A:** _____

6. **Q:** Is there a famous library in Washington, D.C.?   **A:** _____

3 Answer the questions about your town. Give additional information.

1. **Q:** Is there a post office?　　　　　　**A:** _Yes, there's a post office on Main Street._

2. **Q:** Is there a public library?　　　　　　**A:** _____

3. **Q:** Is there a shopping street with lots of stores?　**A:** _____

4. **Q:** Are there any parks?　　　　　　**A:** _____

5. **Q:** Are there any soccer fields?　　　　**A:** _____

6. **Q:** Are there any famous places?　　　　**A:** _____

4 Read the information about Phoenix, Arizona. Write questions and answers. Use *Is there a / an* or *Are there any* and short answers.

Phoenix, Arizona

There are great places to visit in and around Phoenix, Arizona. The weather is sunny almost all year long.

■ South Mountain Park with more than 16,000 acres
■ Heard Museum of traditional Native American art

■ Desert Botanical Garden
■ Phoenix Zoo
■ Children's Museum of Phoenix
■ Grand Canyon tours

1. large park　　　　　　**Q:** _Is there a large park?_ 　**A:** _Yes, there is._

2. Native American art museum　**Q:** _____　**A:** _____

3. botanical garden　　　　**Q:** _____　**A:** _____

4. zoo　　　　　　　　**Q:** _____　**A:** _____

5. Grand Canyon tours　　　**Q:** _____　**A:** _____

6. subway stations　　　　**Q:** _____　**A:** _____

7. children's museum　　　**Q:** _____　**A:** _____

Avoid Common Mistakes

1 Circle the mistakes.

1. **There are** many things to do on Olvera Street. **There is** free tours. **There is** also Latin dancing.
   (a)   (b)   (c)

2. **There is** a nice restaurant in town. **It's** across from my hotel. **There is** popular with tourists.
   (a)   (b)   (c)

3. In Las Vegas, **they're** many famous casinos. **They are** beautiful and **they're** open 24 hours.
                 (a)   (b)   (c)

4. In a college essay: **There's** a famous park in Arizona. **It is** called the Grand Canyon. **There is** great
                       (a)   (b)   (c)
   hiking there.

5. **There are** nice shops downtown. **There are** also some cafés. **There are** one museum.
   (a)   (b)   (c)

6. **They're** many nightclubs in the city. **They're** not expensive. **There is** good music for dancing.
   (a)   (b)   (c)

7. **It's** many national parks in the United States **There are** also state parks. **They are** all popular.
   (a)   (b)   (c)

8. In a college essay: **There is** a shopping mall in my town. **There's** a movie theater inside.
                       (a)   (b)
   It is beautiful.
   (c)

2 Find and correct eight more mistakes in this student essay.

Why I Love Miami

Miami is a wonderful city. ~~There~~ *It* is a great place to shop. There is many well-known stores. Also, they are beautiful white sand beaches. They are very popular with tourists. The beaches are a great place to swim. South Beach is my favorite neighborhood in the city. There is a bright and colorful historic district. They're many restaurants and sidewalk cafés. There is fun places for nightlife. They are concerts. There's something for everybody. Ocean Avenue is a street with many shops and restaurants. There is also many places to stay, including the famous Carlyle Hotel.

Self-Assessment

Circle the word or phrase that correctly completes each sentence.

1. _____ a park and a supermarket on Fifth Street.

   a. There are   b. There is   c. There are no

2. This travel blog is new. _____ comments on it yet.

   a. There is no   b. There aren't any   c. They aren't

3. There is traditional dancing at the festival. _____ very popular with the children.

   a. There is   b. There are   c. It's

4. _____ some beautiful national parks in my country.

   a. There are   b. They're   c. It's

5. **A:** Is there public parking in this area? **B:** Yes, _____ .

   a. there's   b. there is   c. there are

6. **A:** Are there any traditional Italian restaurants near here? **B:** No, _____ .

   a. there aren't some   b. there isn't one   c. there aren't any

7. There are clothing shops in town. _____ on the next street.

   a. There are   b. There is   c. They are

8. _____ a lake in this area?

   a. Is there   b. Are there   c. There is

9. It's a beautiful day. _____ a cloud in the sky.

   a. There are no   b. There isn't   c. Are there

10. _____ one restaurant and many rooms in the hotel.

    a. There are   b. There is   c. It is

11. _____ taxis on the street after midnight.

    a. There are no   b. There is no   c. There isn't

12. There are many traditional foods at the celebration. _____ an important part of the culture.

    a. There are   b. There is   c. They are

13. **A:** Is there a pool at the hotel? **B:** Yes, _____ .

     a. they are   b. there is   c. there's

14. **A:** Are there ocean views from the room? **B:** Yes, _____ from the balcony.

     a. there are one   b. there are some   c. there are any

15. _____ many free museums in Washington, D.C.

     a. There is   b. There isn't   c. There are

Simple Present

Lifestyles

Simple Present: Affirmative and Negative Statements

1 Circle the correct form of the verbs.

1. Americans **live** / **lives** an average of 78 years.

2. An Okinawan **live** / **lives** an average of 82.6 years.

3. Many Americans **have** / **has** a weight problem.

4. They **eat** / **eats** the wrong foods.

5. They **don't exercise** / **doesn't exercise** enough.

6. They **work** / **works** too hard.

7. The younger generation **don't spend** / **doesn't spend** a lot of time at work.

8. In Okinawa, Japan, people **feels** / **feel** close to their families.

9. An Okinawan **walk** / **walks** a lot and **have** / **has** an active life.

2 Complete the sentences. Use the correct affirmative or negative form of the verbs in parentheses.

The Olympic Games _happen_ (happen) once every two years.
(1)

Olympic athletes _____ (train) very hard for these games.
(2)

They _____ (prepare) in many ways. First, athletes _____
(3)   (4)

(eat) very well. They _____ (have) three big meals each day.
(5)

For example, Ryan, a U.S. Olympic swimmer, _____ (eat) a
(6)

12,000 calorie diet every day. He _____ (start) his day with
(7)

eggs, coffee, French toast, and pancakes. For lunch and dinner, he _____ (have) over
(8)

two pounds of pasta, pizza, and energy drinks. He _____ (not miss) a meal.
(9)

Athletes also _____ (exercise) every day. They _____ (not take)
(10)   (11)

much time off. Ryan _____ (swim) for five hours every day. Finally, athletes _____
(12)   (13)

(sleep) at least eight hours each night. They _____ (not stay) up late at night.
(14)

3 Write sentences about Monica and her friends Tom and Johanna. Use the simple present.

1. Monica / work / in a hospital   _Monica works in a hospital._

2. Tom and Johanna / travel / a lot   _____

3. Monica / wake up / at 5:00 a.m.   _____

4. Monica / not eat / breakfast   _____

5. Tom and Johanna / drive / every day   _____

6. Monica / help / patients / in the morning   _____

7. Tom and Johanna / write / travel articles   _____

8. Monica / not go / home / until 6:00 p.m.   _____

4 A Look at the chart. Complete the sentences about the two athletes. ✓ = yes, ✗ = no.

Activity	Jordan Winston – Soccer Player	Viviana Donato – Ice Skater
ice-skate / in the morning	✗	✓
have lunch / at 12:00	✓	✓
practice / in the afternoon	✓	✗
relax at night	✗	✓
visit family / on the weekend	✓	✗
rest / on Sunday	✓	✓
sleep eight hours / every night	✗	✗

1. Viviana _ice-skates_ in the morning.

2. Jordan _doesn't ice skate_ in the morning.

3. Jordan and Viviana _____ at 12:00.

4. Viviana _____ in the afternoon.

5. Viviana _____ at night.

6. Jordan _____ his family on the weekend.

7. Viviana _____ her family on the weekend.

8. Jordan and Viviana _____ on Sunday.

9. Jordan and Viviana _____ eight hours every night.

B Write sentences about what you do and don't do on weekends. Use time expressions.

Do

1. Saturdays and Sundays   *I study on Saturdays and Sundays.*

2. Saturday evenings   _____

3. the afternoon on Sundays   _____

4. the weekend   _____

Don't do

5. Saturday mornings   _____

6. the weekend   _____

7. Sunday mornings   _____

Statements with Adverbs of Frequency

1 Arrange the adverbs of frequency (*sometimes, always, often, rarely, usually, never*) on the scale from 0% to 100% certain.

0%   100%

_____   _____   *sometimes*   _____   _____   _____

2 Use the chart to write sentences about Ms. Parker. Use the adverbs of frequency with check marks (✓).

	Never	Sometimes	Often	Usually	Always
Plan ahead					✓
Begin days without preparation	✓				
Miss meetings	✓				
Be on time for appointments				✓	
Listen to employees					✓
Have coffee with employees			✓		
Learn something new				✓	
Take a 15-minute walk		✓			

1. plan ahead   _Ms. Parker always plans ahead._

2. begin days without preparation   _____

3. miss meetings   _____

4. be on time for appointments   _____

5. listen to employees   _____

6. have coffee with employees   _____

7. learn something new   _____

8. take a 15-minute walk   _____

3 Mario, Elena, Alex, and Lisa manage stress in their lives in different ways. Write sentences about them with the correct form of the verbs. Use adverbs of frequency in the correct position. Sometimes there is more than one correct answer.

1. Mario / do yoga / in the morning / always   _Mario always does yoga in the morning._

2. Elena / listens to / music / sometimes   _____

3. Mario and Elena / be on time for appointments / always   _____

4. Lisa / exercise / at the gym / often   _____

5. Elena / relax / in the evening / usually   _____

6. Lisa and Mario / go to bed late / never   _____

4 Write sentences that are true for you. Use the information below.

1. a good food you often eat   _I often eat fish._

2. a game you sometimes play   _____

3. something you usually do to relax _____

4. something you often think about   _____

5. something you rarely eat   _____

6. a store you never shop at   _____

Avoid Common Mistakes

1 Circle the mistakes.

1. People (stays) healthy in many ways. They **eat** fresh foods. They **get** eight hours of sleep.
     (a)   (b)   (c)

2. My boss **doesn't feels** stressed. Her employees **work** hard, and they **don't get** sick often.
            (a)   (b)   (c)

3. Exercise **is** important for good health. That's why Mary **is swims**, and she **runs**, too.
          (a)   (b)   (c)

4. Robert **is not** a good student. He **doesn't goes** to all his classes, and he **doesn't do**
           (a)   (b)   (c)
his homework.

5. My grandmother **is** 95 years old. She **doesn't eat** meat. She **eat** fruits and vegetables.
              (a)   (b)   (c)

6. John and Katie **are** animal researchers. They **work** in a zoo. They **studies** pandas.
                (a)   (b)   (c)

7. **I'm live** in California near the beach. My wife and I **love** to surf. We **relax** in the water.
     (a)   (b)   (c)

8. Athletes **are** physically active. Their lives **don't be** easy. They **don't have** much time to relax.
          (a)   (b)   (c)

2 Find and correct the mistakes in this article about the Inuit people.

The Inuit People's Diet

The Inuit people ~~lives~~ *live* in Canada, Greenland, Alaska, and Russia.

They are traditional hunters and fishers. They eats whales, seals, polar

bears, and other local animals. The food contain a lot of protein and

fat. They are get an average of 75 percent of their energy from animal

fat. They do not grows plants for food. Instead, the Inuit people eats

grasses, roots, berries, and seaweed. The Inuit people are believes that their diet work better than

Western food. It don't be like a traditional Western diet. The Inuit people feels that their diet is

makes them strong, warm, and full of energy.

Self-Assessment

Circle the word or phrase that correctly completes each sentence.

1. I _____ take vacations in the summer.

    a. don't   b. doesn't   c. am not

2. Sarah _____ a good athlete.

   a. does not be   b. is not   c. do not be

3. Tina and Tim _____ for exercise.

   a. usually dances   b. dance usually   c. usually dance

4. The president has a stressful lifestyle. He _____ often, all over the world.

   a. flys   b. fly   c. flies

5. Older Okinawans _____ exercise in a gym. They are physically active in other ways.

   a. isn't   b. don't   c. doesn't

6. Certain lifestyle habits _____ people live longer.

   a. help   b. helps   c. are help

7. _____ very late at night, and I get tired.

   a. Never I work   b. I often work   c. Always I work

8. Researchers say that healthy children _____ fruits and vegetables.

   a. eat   b. eats   c. is eat

9. On Mondays and Thursdays, I _____ in the pool for one hour.

   a. swims   b. don't be swim   c. swim

10. _____ in the evening. It helps reduce my stress.

   a. I relax always   b. Always I relax   c. I always relax

11. Brian _____ volunteer work. He helps people in other ways.

   a. does not does   b. does not do   c. isn't do

12. Diana _____ a nap in the afternoon.

   a. takes   b. take   c. is take

13. _____ gardening.

   a. Never my parents do   b. My parents do never   c. My parents never do

14. Movies stars _____ houses in expensive areas.

   a. buys   b. buy   c. are buy

15. My brother _____ children during the day.

   a. teach   b. is teach   c. teaches

Simple Present *Yes* / *No* Questions and Short Answers

1 Complete the questions with *Do* or *Does*. Write short or long answers that are true for you.

1. **Q:** (Do) / **Does** you like to cook?   **A:** *No, I don't.* OR *No, I don't like to cook.*

2. **Q:** **Do** / **Does** you have healthy eating habits?   **A:** _____

3. **Q:** **Do** / **Does** your friends eat healthy foods?   **A:** _____

4. **Q:** **Do** / **Does** your friend like vegetables?   **A:** _____

5. **Q:** **Do** / **Does** a family member cook for you?   **A:** _____

6. **Q:** **Do** / **Does** you like to eat fruit?   **A:** _____

7. **Q:** **Do** / **Does** you always eat lunch with friends?   **A:** _____

8. **Q:** **Do** / **Does** your friend like desserts?   **A:** _____

2 Write questions and answers about the Chin family's driving habits. Use *Do* / *Does* and the simple present.

Mrs. Chin   Mr. Chin   Sue Chin

1. Mrs. Chin / wear a seat belt

   Q: *Does Mrs. Chin wear a seat belt?*   **A:** *Yes, she does.*

2. Mr. Chin / use a GPS[1]

   Q: _____   **A:** _____

3. Mr. and Mrs. Chin / talk on their phones

   Q: _____   **A:** _____

[1]**GPS (Global Positioning System):** system that tells you your location and gives directions from place to place

4. Mr. Chin / have a cell phone

Q: _____ A: _____

5. the Chins / wear seat belts

Q: _____ A: _____

6. Sue Chin / text on her phone

Q: _____ A: _____

7. Mrs. Chin and Sue / listen to the radio

Q: _____ A: _____

8. Mrs. Chin and Sue / wear hats

Q: _____ A: _____

3 Complete the questions and answers in this interview on biking habits from *Great Lifestyles* magazine. Use *Do* / *Does* and the simple present.

Lifestyles

Interviewer: Let's talk about the biking habits of people in Denmark. _Do they ride_
(1)
(they / ride) in the cold weather?

Lance Johnson: Yes, _____ . One
(2)
half of the residents in Copenhagen bike to work or school all year long.

Interviewer: _____
(3)
(the city / have) a lot of bike lanes?

Lance Johnson: Yes, _____ . There
(4)
are 350 kilometers of bike lanes in the city. More bike lanes encourage more bike riders.

Interviewer: That's terrific.

_____ (bike riders /
(5)
go out) in any weather?

Lance Johnson: Well, bike riders _____
(6)
(not like) to ride in the rain.

Interviewer: _____
(7)
(the United States / have) bike-friendly cities?

Lance Johnson: Yes, _____ .
(8)
Eugene and Portland in Oregon are two bike-friendly cities on the West Coast.

Interviewer: _____
(9)
(some cities / have) bike-sharing programs?

Lance Johnson: Yes, that's very popular now. People take a bike from one place and leave it in another place. Washington, D.C., and Denver, Colorado, have these programs.

Interviewer: Thanks for your time, Lance. We need more bike-friendly cities. _____
(10)
(you / agree)?

Lance Johnson: Yes, _____ .
(11)

Avoid Common Mistakes

1 Circle the mistakes.

1. **Do you get up** early? **Do you sleep** late? (**Do your sister sleep**) late?
   _(a)   _(b)   _(c)

2. **Do you like** to stay up late? **Do you** a night person? **Do your friends stay up** late?
   _(a)   _(b)   _(c)

3. **Does your teacher drive** a car? **Does she drive** safely? **Is she agree** ?
   _(a)   _(b)   _(c)

4. **Have you** a bike? **Do you ride** it every day? **Do you get** your exercise that way?
   _(a)   _(b)   _(c)

5. **Do you study** with music? **Do your roommate study** with music? **Do you have** an MP3 player?
   _(a)   _(b)   _(c)

6. **Do your driving habits** good? **Do you like** to drive? **Do you have** a car?
   _(a)   _(b)   _(c)

7. **Do you drive** carefully? **Are you take** the highway? **Is the highway** busy?
   _(a)   _(b)   _(c)

8. **Is your car** old? **Are the tires** good? **Does you take** good care of your car?
   _(a)   _(b)   _(c)

2 Find and correct seven more mistakes in this Internet survey.

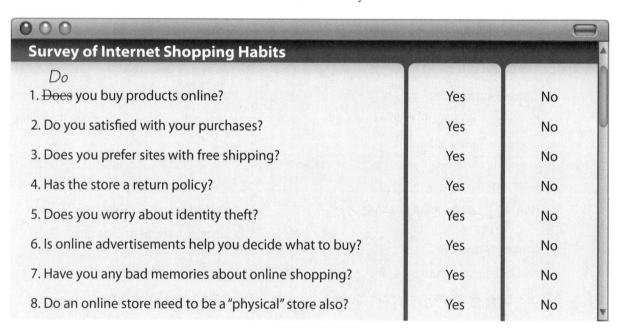

Survey of Internet Shopping Habits

	Yes	No
1. ~~Does~~ *Do* you buy products online?	Yes	No
2. Do you satisfied with your purchases?	Yes	No
3. Does you prefer sites with free shipping?	Yes	No
4. Has the store a return policy?	Yes	No
5. Does you worry about identity theft?	Yes	No
6. Is online advertisements help you decide what to buy?	Yes	No
7. Have you any bad memories about online shopping?	Yes	No
8. Do an online store need to be a "physical" store also?	Yes	No

Self-Assessment

Circle the word or phrase that correctly completes each sentence.

1. _____ banks help you save money?

   a. Do   b. Does   c. Are

2. **A:** Does Mary spend a lot of money on the weekends? **B:** No, _____ .

   a. she isn't   b. she don't   c. she doesn't

3. _____ Chris and Diane study together?

   a. Do   b. Does   c. Are

4. **A:** Do you live in Boston? **B:** _____ .

   a. No, I doesn't   b. No, I'm not   c. No, I don't

5. _____ bicycles popular in Denmark?

   a. Does   b. Are   c. Do

6. _____ people in your home country ride bicycles to work?

   a. Does   b. Do   c. Are

7. _____ safe bike habits?

   a. Have you   b. Has he   c. Do you have

8. **A:** Does the National Sleep Foundation survey people about sleep habits? **B:** Yes, _____ .

   a. it do   b. it is   c. it does

9. _____ ATM cards?

   a. Do your friends have   b. Does your friends have   c. Have your friends

10. _____ the same every week?

    a. Do your schedule   b. Is your schedule   c. Have your schedule

11. _____ good eating habits?

    a. Have most people   b. Do most people have   c. Does most people have

12. _____ remember their dreams?

    a. Do they   b. Does they   c. Have they

13. **A:** Does she have good eating habits? **B:** Yes, _____ .

    a. she does   b. she has   c. she do

14. **A:** Do you dance when you listen to music? **B:** _____ .

    a. Yes, I does   b. No, I doesn't   c. Yes, I do

15. **A:** Do the people in the survey get enough sleep? **B:** No, _____ .

    a. they aren't   b. they doesn't   c. they don't

Simple Present
Information Questions

Cultural Holidays

Simple Present Information Questions

1 Match the questions and answers.

1. **Q:** When do people celebrate Halloween? __e__   a. **A:** To parties and parades.

2. **Q:** What time does the parade begin? _____   b. **A:** Because it is a fun tradition.

3. **Q:** How do people dress on Halloween? _____   c. **A:** Candy.

4. **Q:** Who does the celebration include? _____   d. **A:** They give out candy.

5. **Q:** Where do people go on Halloween? _____   e. **A:** On October 31st.

6. **Q:** What do children get on Halloween? _____   f. **A:** They wear costumes.

7. **Q:** How do people celebrate Halloween? _____   g. **A:** Children and adults.

8. **Q:** Why do people celebrate Halloween? _____   h. **A:** Around 6:00 p.m.

2 Complete the questions in this interview about *Carnaval* in Brazil. Use *who, what, when, where, why,* or *how.*

Susan: Welcome, Fernando. You're here to talk about *Carnaval.* So tell us first, __where__ do people celebrate *Carnaval*?
(1)

Fernando: Well, a lot of countries in Central and South America celebrate *Carnaval.* The biggest celebration is in Brazil.

Susan: _____ do Brazilian people celebrate *Carnaval*?
(2)

Fernando: Because it's a way for people to relax and have fun before the religious month of Lent.

Susan: _____ do people celebrate?
(3)

Fernando: They celebrate with big parades, music, dancing, and parties. Most businesses

close for a week.

Susan: _____ does *Carnaval* begin?
   (4)

Fernando: It usually begins at the end of February or at the beginning of March.

Susan: _____ do people wear?
   (5)

Fernando: A lot of people wear beautiful, colorful costumes.

Susan: _____ do you meet during *Carnaval*?
   (6)

Fernando: You meet tourists from all over the world.

Susan: That's very interesting. Thank you, Fernando.

3 Write questions based on the answers. Use *Who*, *What*, *Where*, *What time*, *How*, *Why*, and *When*.

1. **Q:** Why *do you celebrate the Fourth of July* _____?

   A: We celebrate the Fourth of July because it is the U.S. Independence Day.

2. **Q:** How _____?

   A: We celebrate with parades and barbecues.

3. **Q:** Where _____?

   A: The parades take place in regions all across the country.

4. **Q:** What _____?

   A: Marching bands are in the parades.

5. **Q:** When _____?

   A: We often have the parades in the morning.

6. **Q:** What time _____?

   A: People usually eat around 1:00 or 2:00 p.m.

7. **Q:** What _____?

   A: We eat hamburgers, hot dogs, and salads.

8. **Q:** Why _____?

   A: I like the Fourth of July because the weather is warm.

4 Read the text about birthday celebrations in Mexico. Write information questions and answers based on the information in the text.

Luís is from Mexico. His family has special traditions to celebrate birthdays. On his birthday, they wake him up very early, at 6:00 a.m. They play or sing "Las Mañanitas." It is a traditional birthday song. In the morning, he eats a huge breakfast. On the weekend, his family has a big birthday party. His neighbors, family, and friends come to the party. They dance, eat, and sing until late at night.

Luís's sister, Paola, celebrates her fifteenth birthday this year. They call it the "Quinceañera." This birthday is very important for a teenage girl. It is similar to a "Sweet Sixteen" party for a girl in the United States.

1. **Q:** Where is Luís from?

   A: *He's from Mexico.*

2. **Q:** What time does Luís's family wake him up on his birthday?

   A: _____

3. **Q:** (What) _____

   A: They play or sing "Las Mañanitas."

4. **Q:** What does Luís eat in the morning?

   A: _____

5. **Q:** (When) _____

   A: They have the birthday party on the weekend.

6. **Q:** Who comes to Luís's birthday celebration?

   A: _____

7. **Q:** (Who) _____

   A: Paola celebrates her fifteenth birthday this year.

8. **Q:** (What) _____

   A: A "Quinceañera" is the birthday celebration for a fifteen-year-old girl.

Questions with *How Often*

1 Write questions with *How often* about the Miller family celebrations. Use the information in parentheses to help you.

1. **Q:** (the Miller family / have birthday parties) *How often does the Miller family have birthday parties?*

   A: They have birthday parties three times a year.

2. **Q:** (Jenna / bake a cake) _____

   A: Twice a year. Once for her mother and once for her father.

3. **Q:** (they / buy presents) _____

   A: Several times a year. For the holidays in December, birthdays, and other occasions.

4. **Q:** (they / invite friends to their house) _____

   _____

   A: Every weekend.

5. **Q:** (Mr. Miller / cook for the parties) _____

   _____

   A: Once in a while. Everyone takes turns cooking.

6. **Q:** (they / dance at the parties) _____

   A: All the time. They love to dance.

7. **Q:** (Mrs. Miller / make decorations) _____

   _____

   A: Almost never. She buys decorations instead.

2 Look at the different ways Jun, Eric, and Yelena relax. Write questions with *How often* and the information below. Then answer the questions with the time expressions in the chart.

	Jun	Eric and Yelena
Eat out	three times a month	all the time
See a movie	once a month	every weekend
Read a book	every evening	twice a week
Go to the beach	every other weekend	several times a year
Take a vacation	once a year	almost never

1. Jun / eat out

   Q: _How often does Jun eat out?_   A: _Three times a month._

2. Eric and Yelena / see a movie

   Q: _____   A: _____

3. Jun / read a book

   Q: _____   A: _____

4. Eric and Yelena / go to the beach

   Q: _____   A: _____

5. Jun / take a vacation

   Q: _____   A: _____

6. Eric and Yelena / read a book

   Q: _____   A: _____

7. Jun / go to the beach

   Q: _____   A: _____

8. Eric and Yelena / eat out

   Q: _____   A: _____

3 Write questions with *you* and *How often*. Use the words given. Then answer the questions with information about yourself.

1. go to parties

   Q: _How often do you go to parties?_   A: _About once a month._

2. cook for friends or family

   Q: _____   A: _____

3. invite a friend to dinner

Q: _____   A: _____

4. visit friends

Q: _____   A: _____

5. go to the movies

Q: _____   A: _____

6. read a book

Q: _____   A: _____

Avoid Common Mistakes

1 Circle the mistakes.

1. **When do you** celebrate Independence Day? **What do you** eat that day?
   (a)   (b)
   (Where you) go?
   (c)

2. **Who do we remembers** on Thanksgiving? **Why do we** remember them?
   (a)   (b)
   How do we do it?
   (c)

3. **Why do people** celebrate the Day of the Dead? **Why are they** use symbols?
   (a)   (b)
   What do they mean?
   (c)

4. **Why they** use pictures of the dead? **Where do they** get the skulls?
   (a)   (b)
   What foods do they make?
   (c)

5. Why **do we celebrate** Independence Day in July? What **does it symbolizes**? What
   (a)   (b)
   do we do?
   (c)

6. **When do you** have parades? **Why do you have parades**? **Where you have** the parades?
   (a)   (b)   (c)

7. **How do you** celebrate the New Year? **Who do you** celebrate with?
   (a)   (b)
   What time is it begin?
   (c)

8. When **does Mardi Gras starts**? **Why do we celebrate** it? When
   (a)   (b)
   does the celebration end?
   (c)

2 Find and correct eight more mistakes in this conversation about birthday traditions in India.

Q: How *do* you celebrate birthdays in India?

A: When a child turns one year old, the parents shave the baby's head.

Q: Why they shave the baby's head?

A: It symbolizes people taking away bad energy.

Q: What other traditions is you have for birthdays?

A: We give out chocolates on our birthdays.

Q: Who you give chocolates to?

A: To our classmates in school.

Q: How are people dress on their birthday?

A: A child often wears new, colorful clothes.

Q: What does a family does on a child's birthday?

A: They visit a shrine, and the child receives a blessing.

Q: What else you do?

A: Some families throw rice over the child's head.

Q: Why are they do that?

A: It's a symbol of good luck.

Q: When do you celebrates your birthday?

A: On February 14! It's the same day as Valentine's Day!

Self-Assessment

Circle the word or phrase that correctly completes each sentence.

1. _____ people celebrate Halloween?

   a. Why do   b. Why does   c. Why are

2. Where _____ on Halloween?

   a. does a child goes   b. does a child go   c. is a child go

3. **A:** How do children celebrate Halloween? **B:** _____

   a. In the evening.   b. With candy and costumes.   c. Because it is fun.

4. _____ children receive candy on Halloween?

   a. When does   b. When are   c. When do

5. **A:** _____ on the third Monday in January? **B:** Martin Luther King Jr.

    a. Who do people
       remember
    b. Who do people
       remembers
    c. Who is people
       remember

6. **A:** _____ do they celebrate Martin Luther King Jr.'s birthday? **B:** The third Monday in January.

    a. Where   b. How often   c. When

7. **A:** _____ do we celebrate Martin Luther King Jr.'s birthday? **B:** We celebrate it once a year.

    a. How   b. How often   c. What

8. _____ the Boston Marathon happen?

    a. When does   b. When is   c. When do

9. What time does the race _____?

    a. start   b. starts   c. is start

10. **A:** _____ Brazil celebrate *Carnaval*? **B:** In February or March.

    a. When is   b. When does   c. Why does

11. _____ at *Carnaval*?

    a. What wear people   b. What does people wear   c. What do people wear

12. _____ people have parades and parties during *Carnaval*?

    a. Why   b. Why do   c. Why are

13. **A:** _____ celebrate on January 1? **B:** The New Year.

    a. When do we   b. How often do we   c. What do we

14. **A:** _____ watch on Patriot's Day? **B:** They watch the Boston Marathon.

    a. What do people   b. Where do people   c. How do people

15. When _____ each year?

    a. does Patriot's Day
       takes place
    b. does Patriot's Day
       take place
    c. Patriot's Day
       take place

Conjunctions: *And, But, Or*; *Because*

Time Management

And, But, Or

1 Complete the sentences with *and*, *but*, or *or*.

1. Marco manages his time well **and** / **or** avoids stress.

2. He gets up early **but** / **and** makes breakfast.

3. In the mornings, Marco drives to work **but** / **or** takes the bus.

4. He likes to drive, **or** / **but** sometimes there is too much traffic.

5. When it rains, he takes both a raincoat **and** / **but** an umbrella.

6. He eats lunch at 12:00 **or** / **and** 12:30 every day.

7. He buys his lunch at work with cash **but** / **or** a credit card.

8. He likes his boss, **and** / **or** his boss likes him.

9. He likes his job, **or** / **but** his co-worker does not.

10. Mark works one day each weekend. He works on Saturday **or** / **and** Sunday.

11. On his day off from work, Mark relaxes with his wife **but** / **and** enjoys the time at home.

2 Complete the sentences with *and*, *but*, or *or*.

Ahmed: I work two jobs. I'm very busy night __*and*__ day.
(1)

Frank: Do you prefer your day job _____ your night job?
(2)

Ahmed: I prefer my night job, _____ it is very exhausting.
(3)

Frank: What do you drink at work – coffee _____ tea?
(4)

Ahmed: I usually drink coffee, _____ I like tea occasionally. The break room at work
(5)

usually has both coffee _____ tea available.
(6)

Frank: When do you get home from your night job?

Ahmed: I usually get home at 11:00 p.m., _____ sometimes I get home after midnight.
(7)

Frank: When do you see your family?

Ahmed: I often meet both my brother _____ sister on the weekends. I don't work
(8)

then. I'm always happy to see them.

3 Combine the underlined phrases or sentences with *and*, *but*, or *or*. Add commas where necessary. Use the extra information to help you.

1. She has no free time. **Linh works during the day. / She goes to school at night.**

    Linh works during the day, and she goes to school at night.

2. Her study time is always different. **She does her homework in the morning / at night.**

    _____

3. **During the week, Linh is busy / stressed.**

    _____

4. She sleeps a lot on the weekend. **She wakes up late at 10:00 a.m. / 11:00 a.m.**

    _____

5. **Sometimes Linh goes to work early. / She stays late.** She doesn't stay late when she goes in early.

    _____

6. **Linh's husband leaves every day. / He doesn't go to school.**

    _____

7. He helps Linh with all the housework. **He cooks / buys groceries.**

    _____

8. Her family is very important to her. **Linh is very busy. / She also makes time for her family.**

    _____

Because

1 **A** Read the sentence pairs. Put *C* for cause and *E* for effect.

1. _E_ Sonia has good grades.

   _C_ Sonia studies every day.

2. ____ She plans her time well.

   ____ She finishes all her tasks.

3. ____ Sonia's friend Raj sleeps late.

   ____ Raj doesn't get to work on time.

4. ____ They spend time together on the weekends.

   ____ They don't have time to see each other during the week.

5. ____ Sonia and her parents live in different states.

   ____ They do not see each other often.

6. ____ Sonia doesn't have time to cook in the evening.

   ____ She works late all week.

B Combine the sentence pairs in A. Use *because*. Write the sentences in two ways.

1. *Sonia has good grades because she studies every day.*

   Because Sonia studies every day, she has good grades.

2. _____

   _____

3. _____

   _____

4. _____

   _____

   _____

   _____

5. _____

   _____

6. _____

   _____

2 Check the correct answer for each question. Then write full sentences. Use *because* and a comma where necessary.

1. Why does Tara study English?

   __✓__ Because she wants to go to school in Canada.   _____ Because she speaks Spanish.

   Tara studies English because she wants to go to school in Canada.

2. Why does she want to study in Canada?

   _____ Because her friends and family are there.   _____ Because she doesn't like Canada.

   _____

3. Why does she get up early?

   _____ Because her job starts at 8:00 a.m.   _____ Because she has school at night.

   _____

4. Why does she make a "to do" list every day?

   _____ Because she is tired.   _____ Because she has a busy schedule.

   _____

5. Why does Tara work so hard?

   _____ Because she wants to save money for school in Canada.   _____ Because she goes to work.

   _____

3 Answer the questions with information that is true for you. Use *because* in your answers.

1. Are you an organized person? Why or why not?

   Yes, I am an organized person because I plan every day.

2. Are your friends organized? Why or why not?

   _____

3. Why do you go to school?

   _____

4. Do you have extra time for leisure activities? Why or why not?

   _____

Avoid Common Mistakes

1 Circle the mistakes.

1. Organized people plan their (day,) and make a list. They feel **better and avoid** stress.
   (a)   (b)   (c)

2. I get up early**,** **because I work at 7:00 a.m.** I don't work at night **because I am tired**.
            (a)   (b)   (c)

3. **Because** Maria is always **on time,** she gets her work done. She does her tasks quickly **or** correctly.
       (a)   (b)   (c)

4. **Because** her job is busy**,** Tara writes her tasks. She types them in an e-mail **but** reads it the next day.
       (a)   (b)   (c)

5. **Because** she is very **busy** Maria is never home. She is at work **or** at school.
       (a)   (b)   (c)

6. John wants to **exercise** but **he** doesn't have time to do it. He belongs to a gym **but** does not go.
                     (a)   (b)   (c)

7. I **create a list and** check it often. **Because I never forget my tasks,** the list helps me.
      (a)   (b)   (c)

8. I get up at 6:00, **and** my wife gets up at 7:00. After breakfast, we make a **list, and** plan our day.
                  (a)   (b)   (c)

2 Find and correct eight more mistakes in the article about parents and school.

Today's Parents

Today more adults work, and go to school at the same time. They work or study, and they raise children, too. They prepare meals for their families, help their kids with homework, but study. Some parents make a "to do" list, because it helps them organize their busy day. Because they have many responsibilities, they use several ways to control their stress. Most parents take classes at night, on the weekends, but online. The children are still asleep because some parents get up early to study. Other parents study after the children are in bed or they study on the weekend. Because they plan carefully many parents do well with work, and school. It is not easy, but many parents do it.

Self-Assessment

Circle the word or phrase that correctly completes each sentence.

1. You are either an organized person _____ a disorganized person.

   a. and   b. or   c. but

2. Because Nina makes a "to do" _____ she has time to relax every day.

   a. list,   b. list.   c. list

3. Put the task on the calendar feature on your phone, _____ don't forget to do it.

   a. or   b. but   c. because

4. Robert arrives late _____ he doesn't like to get up early.

   a. for work. Because   b. for work, because   c. for work because

5. Joe doesn't study very much, _____ his grades are very good.

   a. and   b. or   c. but

6. Richard has time to relax at night _____ his work done early.

   a. because he gets   b. because gets   c. because

7. I wear jeans _____ nice pants to work.

   a. and   b. or   c. but

8. Ray has _____ he doesn't have time to spend it.

   a. money, but   b. money but   c. money, or

9. Some parents go to work during the day _____ see their children at night.

   a. because   b. or   c. and

10. _____ Sue works Monday through Friday, she takes classes on Saturday.

    a. But   b. Because   c. Because,

11. I have a lot of meetings _____ tasks to do at work every day.

    a. or   b. but   c. and

12. Because Peter works seven days a _____ doesn't have time to go to school.

    a. week. He   b. week, he   c. week he

13. I like to be _____ I am often late.

    a. on time, but   b. on time but   c. on time and

14. I ride my bike to work, _____ I take the bus.

    a. and   b. but   c. or

15. Some people feel _____ they are disorganized.

    a. stressed. Because   b. stressed, because   c. stressed because

Simple Past Statements

Success Stories

Simple Past Statements: Regular Verbs

1 Read the success story of Neil Armstrong. Complete the sentences with simple past form of the verbs in parentheses.

Neil Armstrong is a famous American astronaut. As a

boy, he __*lived*__ (live) with his family in Ohio. Young Neil
(1)

_____ (love) airplanes. He and his father
(2)

_____ (visit) the airport many times. There,
(3)

he _____ (watch) planes take off and land.
(4)

During high school, Neil _____ (work) to make
(5)

money for flying lessons. He _____ (receive) his
(6)

private pilot's license when he was 16 years old. At that time,

Neil _____ (not learn) to drive a car, but he
(7)

_____ (learn) to fly a plane.
(8)

In 1962, Neil and many other people _____ (apply) to NASA
(9)

to be astronauts. NASA _____ (not accept) everyone, but they
(10)

_____ (accept) Neil. In 1966, Neil _____ (travel) into space
(11)   (12)

for the first time on *Gemini 8*. In January of 1969, NASA _____ (ask) Neil
(13)

to be the commander of *Apollo 11*, the first mission to the moon. Finally, on July 20, 1969,

Apollo 11 _____ (land) on the moon. When Neil _____
(14)   (15)

(return) home, the country _____ (honor) him as a national hero.
(16)

2 Complete the sentences about Linda's successful job search. Put the verbs in parentheses in the simple past. Use correct spelling.

1. In college, Linda _*didn't study*_ (not study) once a week.

   She _*studied*_ (study) every day.

2. Linda _____ (not want) a new car after college.

   She _____ (want) a good job.

3. Linda _____ (not plan) her schedule.

   She _____ (plan) her future.

4. Her adviser _____ (not refer) her to a company in Chicago.

   He _____ (refer) her to a company in New York City.

5. Linda _____ (not apply) to a small company.

   She _____ (apply) to a big company.

6. The company _____ (not invite) her to a party.

   They _____ (invite) her for an interview.

7. She _____ (not travel) to Chicago.

   She _____ (travel) to New York.

8. She _____ (not stay) in an apartment.

   She _____ (stay) in a hotel.

9. The next day, the interview _____ (not start) late.

   It _____ (start) on time.

10. The company _____ (not offer) her a new house.

    They _____ (offer) her a new job.

11. Linda _____ (not decide) to stay in her hometown.

    She _____ (decide) to move to New York City for the job.

3 Write affirmative and negative sentences about Steve Jobs, the co-founder of Apple. Use the simple past.

1. Steve Jobs / live in California / as a child   _Steve Jobs lived in California as a child._

2. He / not like / team sports   _____

3. He / work / independently   _____

4. His father / fix cars / as a hobby   _____

5. Steve / attend / Reed College in 1972   _____

6. He / not finish / college   _____

7. He / travel / to India   _____

8. He / not stay / in India long   _____

9. He / return / to California   _____

10. He and his friend Steve Wozniak / attend / computer club meetings   _____

    _____

11. Steve Jobs and Steve Wozniak / form / Apple in 1976   _____

    _____

12. The company / earn / over $200 million in three years   _____

    _____

4 Write affirmative and negative sentences in the simple past about things you or your friends did last week. Use the verbs given.

1. play   _My friend and I played soccer last week._

2. not walk   _____

3. study   _____

4. not shop   _____

5. watch   _____

6. not visit _____

7. call _____

8. not open _____

Simple Past Statements: Irregular Verbs

1 Complete the sentences with affirmative and negative irregular simple past verbs.

Alexander Graham Bell _grew up_ (1) (grow up) in Scotland. He _____ (2) (have) two brothers, but he _____ (3) (not have) sisters. His father _____ (4) (become) a well-known teacher of hearing impaired[1] people. His grandfather _____ (5) (write) books to help people speak better. As a child, Alexander invented things. Often, his inventions _____ (6) (go) wrong, but he _____ (7) (not give up).

Years later, his family _____ (8) (leave) Scotland for Canada. A few years later, he _____ (9) (go) to Boston. He _____ (10) (get) a job as a teacher. Like his father, he _____ (11) (teach) hearing impaired people. At school, he _____ (12) (meet) Mabel Hubbard, one of his students. They _____ (13) (fall) in love. They _____ (14) (become) closer and married a few years later.

Alexander _____ (15) (make) the first telephone in 1876. He _____ (16) (begin) a business called the Bell Telephone Company. It _____ (17) (sell) many telephones. By 1917, most of the United States _____ (18) (have) phone service.

_____
[1]**hearing impaired:** having problems hearing or unable to hear

2 Each sentence below is incorrect. Change the negative statements to affirmative and change the affirmative statements to negative to write true facts about Roberto Clemente.

1. Roberto Clemente did not become a successful baseball player.

   FACT: *Roberto Clemente became a successful baseball player.*

2. He grew up in a small family.

   FACT: *He didn't grow up in a small family.*

3. His parents made a lot of money.

   FACT: _____

4. He didn't get a part-time job to help his family.

   FACT: _____

5. At age 20, Roberto didn't come to Pittsburgh to play baseball.

   FACT: _____

6. He spoke English.

   FACT: _____

7. He got married in California.

   FACT: _____

8. In 1960, Roberto's team didn't win the baseball World Series.

   FACT: _____

9. In 1971, sports reporters didn't give Roberto a special honor.

   FACT: _____

10. He didn't lose his life in a plane crash a year later.

    FACT: _____

3 Write sentences in the simple past.

1. Alberto / come / to Canada / from Mexico   *Alberto came to Canada from Mexico.*

2. He / go / to a small college   _____

3. He / sing / in a band   _____

4. After college / he / meet / his friend Jun   _____

5. Jun / have / a small record company   _____

6. Jun / give / Alberto / a record deal   _____

7. Alberto / become / a famous musician   _____

8. Alberto and Jun / get / rich   _____

4 Write sentences about success stories that you know about. Use the simple past form of the verbs. You can use your own ideas or information from this unit and in the Student's Book.

1. grow up   *Neil Armstrong grew up in Ohio.*

2. become   _____

3. have   _____

4. go   _____

5. make   _____

6. see   _____

Avoid Common Mistakes

1 Circle the mistakes.

1. The Beatles **come** to the United States in 1964. They **received** a big welcome. People
   (a)   (b)
   loved them.
   (c)

2. Emily Dickinson **lived** in the 1800s. She **wrote** many poems. She **didn't used** correct
   (a)   (b)   (c)
   punctuation.

3. She **didnot publish** many poems in her lifetime. Emily **became** famous after she died.
   (a)   (b)   (c)

4. I **needed** help with English. I **asked** my friend. He **had not** time to help me.
   (a)   (b)   (c)

5. I **did not** my report on time, but my teacher **accepted** it late. I **got** a good grade.
   (a)   (b)   (c)

6. Abraham Lincoln **didn't win** his first election. He **didn't give up**. He **try** again.
   (a)   (b)   (c)

7. Thomas Edison **did not** stay in school long. He **droped** out, but he **continued** to learn.
   (a)   (b)   (c)

8. Thomas Edison **invent** the first lightbulb. His invention **became** popular. It **helped**
   (a)   (b)   (c)
   many people.

2 Find and correct eight more mistakes.

              come
Ana did not ~~came~~ from a rich family. Her parents didnot finish high school. She always

studyed hard in school. In 1989, Ana takes college classes.

At first, she did not very well. She had problems with math and English, but she loved

to learn. She asked her teachers and friends for help. Her grades got better quickly. She

graduated from college. Her family had not money for a big party, but they were very

proud. She didn't ended her education there. Three years later, Ana goes to medical school.

She becomes a doctor. She worked with sick children. Everyone in her town knew her and

respected her. Today, Ana is still a doctor, and she helps girls who want to become doctors.

Self-Assessment

Circle the word or phrase that correctly completes each sentence.

1. Albert Einstein _____ science and math.

   a. study   b. studyed   c. studied

2. He _____ his work in school.

   a. did not do   b. did not   c. didnot do

3. The Beatles _____ a contract with a record company.

   a. sign   b. signed   c. didn't signed

4. They _____ very popular around the world.

   a. become   b. did not became   c. became

5. Their record company _____ them a lot of money.

   a. pay   b. paid   c. payed

6. An executive _____ that The Beatles had talent.

   a. thought   b. thinked   c. thoughts

7. The band manager _____ the money.

   a. controled   b. controld   c. controlled

8. In 1952, Roberto Clemente _____ many fans.

   a. did not had   b. had not   c. didn't have

9. In 1960, baseball fans _____ Roberto Clemente.

   a. loved   b. love   c. did not loved

10. Alexander Graham Bell _____ in the United States.

    a. did not grew up   b. grow up   c. did not grow up

11. Alexander _____ hearing impaired people.

    a. teached   b. teaches   c. taught

12. He _____ vision impaired students.

    a. didnot have   b. had not   c. did not have

13. Alexander _____ the lightbulb.

    a. did not invent   b. invents   c. did not invented

14. NASA _____ Neil Armstrong to go to the moon.

    a. permitted   b. permited   c. permit

15. Emily Dickinson _____ newspaper articles.

    a. did not wrote   b. didnot write   c. did not write

Simple Past Questions

Business Ideas

Simple Past *Yes / No* Questions

1 Complete the *Yes / No* questions with the simple past. Then write short answers based on the information in the paragraphs.

Tom Warth grew up in England. He came to the United States in 1960. He started a book business in Minnesota. In the 1970s, his company expanded. He sold many books. In 1989, a publishing company bought his business.

1. **Q:** (Tom / grow up) _Did Tom grow up_ _____ in England?

   A: _Yes, he did._ _____

2. **Q:** (He / come) _____ to the United States in 1980?

   A: _____

3. **Q:** (He / start) _____ a book business in Minnesota?

   A: _____

4. **Q:** (His company / expand) _____ in the 1960s?

   A: _____

5. **Q:** (He / sell) _____ many books?

   A: _____

Tom didn't want to retire. He traveled to Uganda. He saw a library with no books, so he began a new company. He called the new company Books for Africa. He collected old books from people and schools in Minnesota. He shipped the books to Africa. By 2010, Books for Africa distributed over 23 million books in 45 African countries.

6. **Q:** (He / travel) _____ to Uganda?

   A: _____

7. **Q:** (He / see) _____ a library with many books?

   A: _____

8. **Q:** (He / collect) _____ old shoes?

   A: _____

9. **Q:** (He / ship) _____ books to Africa?

   A: _____

10. **Q:** (Books for Africa / distribute) _____ over 23 million books in Africa?

   A: _____

2 Write simple past *Yes / No* questions about a community college graduate. Use the answers to help you.

1. **Q:** (Margi / study / nursing) *Did Margi study nursing?* _____

   A: Yes, she studied nursing at Gateway Community College.

2. **Q:** (her teachers / give / homework) _____

   A: Yes, all her teachers gave a lot of homework.

3. **Q:** (she / like / all her teachers) _____

   A: No, she didn't like all her teachers.

4. **Q:** (Margi / graduate) _____

   A: Yes, Margi graduated with honors.

5. **Q:** (she / transfer / to a university) _____

   A: No, she didn't transfer to a university right away.

6. **Q:** (she / begin / a job) _____

   A: Yes, she began a job in a hospital after graduation.

7. **Q:** (she / start / at a university) _____

   A: Yes, she started at a university three years later.

8. **Q:** (she / look / for a new job) _____

   A: No, she didn't. She started her own business for nurses.

9. **Q:** (the nurses / visit / older patients) _____

   A: Yes, the nurses visited older patients in their homes.

10. **Q:** (her business / succeed) _____

   A: Yes, it did. Her nurses provided excellent care.

3 Write simple past *Yes / No* questions for the statements about Mark Zuckerberg, the creator of Facebook.

1. Mark studied at Harvard.

   Did Mark study at Harvard?

2. Mark started a social networking site.

   _____

3. The site expanded to other universities.

   _____

4. The concept grew quickly.

   _____

5. It became Facebook.com in 2005.

   _____

6. The site opened to everyone in 2006.

   _____

7. Some countries blocked the site.

   _____

8. Some companies did not allow employees to use Facebook.com.

   _____

4 Interview a successful person in your life. Write simple past *Yes / No* questions and short answers.

1. go / to college   Q: *Did you go to college?*   A: *Yes, I did.*

2. start / a business   Q: _____   A: _____

3. have / an office   Q: _____   A: _____

4. travel / abroad   Q: _____   A: _____

5. meet / new friends   Q: _____   A: _____

6. learn / new skills   Q: _____   A: _____

Simple Past Information Questions

1 Write simple past information questions about Carol Bartz, a former CEO (Chief Executive Officer) of Yahoo. Use the information below.

1. where / Carol Bartz / live as a child

   Q: _Where did Carol Bartz live as a child?_   **A:** Minnesota.

2. who / she / help / care for

   Q: _____   **A:** Her brother.

3. where / Carol / move

   Q: _____   **A:** A farm in Wisconsin.

4. why / Carol and her brother / live with their grandmother

   Q: _____   **A:** Because their mother died.

5. what / she / like in high school

   Q: _____   **A:** Math.

6. when / she / graduate from college

   Q: _____   **A:** In 1971.

7. what / she / do well in

   Q: _____   **A:** Business classes.

8. who / the company Yahoo! / hire as their new CEO

   Q: _____   **A:** Carol.

2 Write simple past information questions about a Nobel Peace Prize winner. Use the answers to help you.

1. **Q:** Where _did Muhammad Yunus grow up_ ?

   A: Muhammad Yunus grew up **in Bangladesh**.

2. **Q:** What _____ ?

   A: He started **a bank** for poor people.

3. **Q:** Who _____ ?

   A: The bank helped **poor people in Bangladesh**.

4. **Q:** When _____ ?

   A: He opened the bank **in 1976**.

5. **Q:** How _____ ?

   A: Borrowers returned the money **slowly**.

6. **Q:** Where _____ ?

   A: The bank expanded **to other parts of Bangladesh**.

7. **Q:** Why _____ ?

   A: Muhammad won the Nobel Peace Prize **because** he helped people.

8. **Q:** Who _____ ?

   A: The people loved **Muhammad**.

3 A Write simple past information questions about Ana's professional profile using the words given and the verbs in the profile. Then write the answers.

Professional Profile · Ana Lopez

2000	Studied hairstyling
2001	Worked in a hair salon
2005	Moved to Hollywood for more opportunities
2006	Helped famous clients with their hairstyles
2009	Opened her own hair salon

1. what / in 2000

   Q: _What did Ana study in 2000?_   **A:** _Hairstyling._

2. where / in 2001

   Q: _____   **A:** _____

3. why / in 2005

   Q: _____   **A:** _____

4. who / in 2006

   Q: _____   **A:** _____

5. when / open her own hair salon

   Q: _____   **A:** _____

B Now help someone you know prepare to write his or her profile. Write simple past information questions and answers.

1. what / study in college

   Q: _What did you study in college?_   A: _Medicine._

2. when / start your job

   Q: _____   A: _____

3. where / work

   Q: _____   A: _____

4. why / choose / this career

   Q: _____   A: _____

Avoid Common Mistakes

1 Circle the mistakes.

1. (**When you finish**) nursing school? **Where did you** study? **Why did you** choose nursing?
   ⎵(a)⎵   (b)   (c)

2. Where did Blake **distributed** shoes? Who did he **give** them to? How did he **distribute** them?
                    (a)   (b)   (c)

3. What **did you see** at the trade show? Who **did you go** with? How **was you got** there?
        (a)   (b)   (c)

4. How **did you develop** the concept? Why **did the concept** well? Who **did it help**?
       (a)   (b)   (c)

5. When **did you start** your business? **Did it had** many customers? How **did you advertise**?
        (a)   (b)   (c)

6. Why **you studied** business? **Did you open** your own company? **Did your company expand**?
       (a)   (b)   (c)

7. **What did you** with your business? **Did you sell** your business? **Why did you** sell your business?
   (a)   (b)   (c)

8. When **did Muhammad open** the bank? Who **the bank serve**? **Did it help** people?
        (a)   (b)   (c)

2 Find and correct seven more mistakes in this interview with the owner of a popular smoothie store.

did   get

Interviewer: Where you ~~got~~ the concept for your smoothie stores?

Owner: When I was a child, my mother made me smoothies.

Interviewer: Did you liked her smoothies? When she made them?

Owner: I loved them! She made them every day!

Interviewer: Did you had a favorite?

Owner: Yes, my favorite was strawberry with bananas.

Interviewer: Why you wanted to start a smoothie business?

Owner: Because I knew they were easy and delicious.

Interviewer: When did you started your first smoothie store? Where it opened?

Owner: I opened it in 1997 in my hometown, and people liked it right away.

Interviewer: What did you to expand the business?

Owner: I opened more stores. Today, I have over 100 smoothie stores around the country.

Self-Assessment

Circle the word or phrase that correctly completes each sentence.

1. _____ a business with his sister?

   a. Did Andrew start   b. Was Andrew start   c. Did Andrew started

2. How _____ you with your business concept?

   a. was your friends help   b. your friends helped   c. did your friends help

3. **A:** Did the manager become a millionaire? **B:** _____ .

   a. No, he did   b. No, he wasn't   c. No, he didn't

4. _____ Blake a social entrepreneur?

   a. Why did people call   b. Why did people called   c. Why people call

5. **A:** _____ did customers like Pinkberry? **B:** Because the yogurt wasn't too sweet.

   a. What   b. Who   c. Why

6. Where _____ her first clothing store?

   a. your sister open   b. did your sister open   c. did your sister opened

7. **A:** _____ did you start your business? **B:** I it in 2008.

   a. Where   b. When   c. What

8. **A:** _____? **B:** Yes, she did.

   a. Did Carol do well   b. What did Carol do   c. Why did Carol well
      in business   well in   in business

9. Who _____ as their new CEO last year?

   a. the company choose   b. did the company chose   c. did the company choose

10. _____ accounting?

    a. your friend studied   b. Was your friend studied   c. Did your friend study

11. _____ the idea for Facebook.com?

    a. Where did Mark get   b. Where did Mark got   c. Where Mark got

12. _____ to other universities?

    a. Did you applied   b. Did apply you   c. Did you apply

13. When _____ popular?

    a. did social networking   b. was social networking   c. did social networking
       became   became   become

14. _____ in your computer class?

    a. What did students   b. What did students do   c. What was students do

15. Why _____ her own clothing design company?

    a. did Lisa had   b. was Lisa had   c. did Lisa have

Simple Past of *Be*
Life Stories

Simple Past of *Be*: Affirmative and Negative Statements

1 Circle the correct simple past form of *be* in the sentences about Brad Pitt's childhood.

1. Brad Pitt **was** / **were** born on December 18, 1963.

2. He **was not** / **were not** born in California.

3. Brad **was not** / **were not** one of five children.

4. Doug and Julie Pitt **was** / **were** his brother and sister.

5. His parents **was** / **were** hard workers.

6. They **was not** / **were not** lawyers.

7. His mother **was** / **were** a school counselor.

8. His brother and sister **was not** / **were not** older than him.

9. Brad **was** / **were** popular in high school.

10. Brad's college major **was** / **were** journalism.

11. In 1987, his parts in movies **was not** / **were not** big.

12. His first big movie role **was** / **were** in *A River Runs Through It*.

2 Complete the sentences with *was*, *were*, *wasn't*, or *weren't*.

Dolly Parton __was__ born in 1946 in Tennessee. Her childhood
                (1)

_____ (not) easy. Her family _____ loving and supportive, but
   (2)   (3)

they _____ (not) rich. Dolly _____ the fourth child of twelve. The
        (4)   (5)

family home _____ very small. Because Dolly's family was poor, her
               (6)

mother made her a coat from rags. The rags _____ many different
                                              (7)

colors. When Dolly wore the coat to school, the children laughed at her.

Dolly's father _____ (not) a guitar player, but her mother _____ . When Dolly
                  (8)   (9)

was seven years old, her uncle bought her a guitar. She learned to play it. Dolly _____
                                                                                    (10)

a very good singer.

By age ten, Dolly _____ on a local TV show. She recorded her first song as a teenager.
(11)

Her songs _____ popular. She eventually moved to Nashville for her musical career after
(12)

high school. Today, Dolly is one of the most successful singers in the music business.

3 Look at the facts below about Michelle Obama's childhood. Write negative statements with *was not* and *were not*. Then write affirmative statements with *was* and *were* and the information in parentheses.

1. Michelle Obama / born in Hawaii (Chicago)

   Michelle Obama was not born in Hawaii. She was born in Chicago.

2. Michelle / in regular classes. (honors classes)

3. Michelle and her brother/ lazy (hard workers)

4. Michelle / the oldest child (the youngest)

5. Michelle and her brother / twins (just under two years apart)

6. Her parents / born in the 1940s (the 1930s)

7. Michelle and her brother / poor students (intelligent students)

8. Michelle's major / chemistry (sociology)

9. Her father / a doctor (city employee)

10. Michelle / a law student in 1978 (1988)

4 Write sentences about your childhood. Use *was* and *were*.

1. Your best friends: <u>My best friends were Ana and Lily.</u>

2. Your favorite sport: _____

3. Your place of birth: _____

4. Your favorite foods: _____

5. Your favorite color: _____

6. Your favorite subject: _____

7. Your favorite teacher: _____

8. Your favorite animal: _____

Simple Past of *Be*: Questions and Answers

1 Complete the *Yes / No* questions about your childhood with *was*, *were*, *wasn't*, or *weren't*. Write short answers that are true for you.

1. **Q:** <u>Were</u> you born in the United States? **A:** <u>No, I wasn't.</u>

2. **Q:** _____ your classmates friendly? **A:** _____

3. **Q:** _____ your teachers helpful? **A:** _____

4. **Q:** _____ your family big? **A:** _____

5. **Q:** _____ your home small? **A:** _____

6. **Q:** _____ you a shy child? **A:** _____

7. **Q:** _____ your favorite color blue? **A:** _____

8. **Q:** _____ your best friend funny? **A:** _____

9. **Q:** _____ your school far from your home? **A:** _____

10. **Q:** _____ you a student in 2009? **A:** _____

11. **Q:** _____ you a college student in another country? **A:** _____

12. **Q:** _____ your high school classes easy? **A:** _____

2 Read about John, a man who grew up in Alaska. Complete the questions with *was* and *were*. Then write short answers based on his autobiography.

I grew up in Alaska in the 1940s. Life was difficult back then. We didn't have a lot of things that people have today, such as cars. Cars weren't common where I lived. The best way to travel was by small plane or boat.

Though there were very few roads, the Alaska Highway made it possible to travel by car from Alaska to other U.S. states. Back then, Alaska wasn't considered a state. It didn't become a state until 1959. This was probably because of its tiny population. The population of Alaska in 1940 was just over 72,000 people.

With so few people, Alaska was very quiet and peaceful. However, my family and I were never bored. Sometimes we went ice skating in the winter. Many people think that the days are always cold and dark in Alaska. However, in our summers, we had 24-hour daylight, and it wasn't cold.

1. **Q:** _*Was*_ life difficult in Alaska in the 1940s?   **A:** _____

2. **Q:** _____ cars a part of daily life?   **A:** _____

3. **Q:** _____ the best way to travel by bus and train?   **A:** _____

4. **Q:** _____ you and your family bored there?   **A:** _____

5. **Q:** _____ the days always cold and dark?   **A:** _____

6. **Q:** _____ the population big in the state at that time?   **A:** _____

7. **Q:** _____ it possible to travel by car from other U.S. states to Alaska?   **A:** _____

8. **Q:** _____ Alaska a state in the 1940s?   **A:** _____

3 Write questions to ask John more about his childhood in Alaska. Use the answers to help you form the questions.

1. **Q:** (When) _When were you born?_   **A:** I was born **in 1937**.

2. **Q:** (Where) _____   **A:** My family's home was **in Nome, Alaska**.

3. **Q:** (What time) _____   **A:** My classes were **at 7:00** every morning.

4. **Q:** (What) _____   **A:** My parents' names were **Joe and Linda**.

5. **Q:** (How) _____   **A:** The weather was **cold, windy, and snowy**.

6. **Q:** (What) _____   **A:** My favorite animal there was **the polar bear**.

7. **Q:** (Who) _____   **A:** My friends were **native Alaskans**.

8. **Q:** (Why) _____   **A:** I was happy there **because I loved nature** as a child.

4 Ask a friend about an important event in his or her childhood. Write information questions and *Yes / No* questions. Use the information in parentheses. Then write true answers.

1. **Q:** (what / the event) _What was the event?_ _____

   A: _The event was a surprise party for my sister._ _____

2. **Q:** (when / the event) _____

   A: _____

3. **Q:** (your family / present) _Was your family present?_ _____

   A: _____

4. **Q:** (who else / present) _____

   A: _____

5. **Q:** (it / exciting) _____

   A: _____

6. **Q:** (why / the event important) _____

   A: _____

7. **Q:** (the event / outside) _____

   A: _____

8. **Q:** (you / happy) _____

   A: _____

Avoid Common Mistakes

1 Circle the mistakes.

1. **He was born** in Paris. (**His parents born**) in London. **His family was** small.
   ‎ (a) ‎ (b) ‎ (c)

2. **How old were they** two years ago? **They was** 19 years old. **Was their friend** 19, too?
   ‎ (a) ‎ (b) ‎ (c)

3. **Bill Gates was** from a typical family. **His father was** a lawyer. **His mother were not**
   ‎ (a) ‎ (b) ‎ (c)
   a doctor.

4. Where **were Bill born**? **Was he born** in New York? **Was he** a smart child?
   ‎ (a) ‎ (b) ‎ (c)

5. **What was** important to Bill? **Was computers** important? **Where was** his computer lab?
   ‎ (a) ‎ (b) ‎ (c)

6. **Bill were** active and busy. **He was** bored in school. **He and his friends were** interested
   ‎ (a) ‎ (b) ‎ (c)
   in software.

7. **Your mother born** in 1950? Where **were you born**? **Were you six** when you
   ‎ (a) ‎ (b) ‎ (c)
   started school?

8. **Penelope Cruz not born** in New York. **Her parents were not** lawyers. **She was**
   ‎ (a) ‎ (b) ‎ (c)
   talented.

2 Read the study guide for a history quiz. Correct eight more mistakes in the questions and answers.

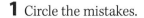

1. When *was* George Washington born?   He born in 1732.

2. Was his family large?   Yes, seven brothers and sisters was in the family.

3. When was his mother born?   She born in 1708.

4. Who were his parents?   They was Augustine Washington and Mary Ball.

5. Was his parents poor?   His parents were not poor.

6. Was his father a banker?   His father were not a banker. He was a landowner.

7. How old was George when his father died?   He were 11 years old.

8. Why didn't George join the Royal Navy at age 15?   Because his mother were sad and did not want him to leave.

Self-Assessment

Circle the word or phrase that correctly completes each sentence.

1. _____ in Madrid, Spain, in 1974?

   a. Who was born   b. Was born   c. Who born

2. _____ in many movies as a child.

   a. Was Penelope Cruz   b. Penelope Cruz were   c. Penelope Cruz was

3. **A:** Was Brad Pitt born in 1963? **B:** _____ .

   a. No, he weren't   b. Yes, he was   c. Yes, he were

4. _____ popular in high school?

   a. Brad was   b. Was Brad   c. Brad

5. _____ Taylor Swift shy as a child?

   a. What was   b. Why was   c. Who was

6. _____ a songwriter and singer in high school.

   a. Taylor Swift were   b. Was   c. Taylor Swift was

7. _____ very simple and plain.

   a. My grandmother's   b. My grandmother's   c. My grandmother's
   house was   house were   house

8. _____ in Chicago?

   a. Her parents born   b. Were her parents born   c. Was her parents born

9. Michelle Obama _____ a bad student.

   a. not was   b. was not   c. weren't

10. _____ active volunteers in their community?

    a. Were Michelle and   b. Was Michelle and   c. Michelle and her
    her brother   her brother   brother were

11. **A:** Was Dolly the fourth of 12 children? **B:** _____ .

    a. Yes, she were   b. No, she weren't   c. Yes, she was

12. **A:** _____ was she born? **B:** At 6:00 a.m.

    a. Who   b. What   c. What time

13. Dolly wore a coat of rags. _____ many different colors.

    a. The rags were   b. Was the rags   c. The rags was

14. Dolly and her brothers and sisters _____ good at music.

    a. was   b. was not   c. were

15. **A:** _____ a successful singer? **B:** Because she was very talented.

    a. Why she was   b. How was she   c. Why was she

Past Time Clauses with *When, Before,* and *After*

Luck and Loss

Past Time Clauses with *When, Before,* and *After*

1 Read the sentences. Underline the time clauses, and number the events to show which action happened first and which happened second.

1. When I got home from my office last night, I made dinner.

   Event __1__   Event __2__

2. Before I sat down for dinner, I saw an offer for a free printer on TV.

   Event _____   Event _____

3. When they showed the phone number, I called it.

   Event _____   Event _____

4. The woman explained the offer before I asked any questions.

   Event _____   Event _____

5. Before I made a decision, I learned that the shipping fee was $100.

   Event _____   Event _____

6. After I learned that, I said good-bye.

   Event _____   Event _____

2 Read the sentences about a woman who took a taxi in New York City. Then circle the correct words to complete the sentences.

1. **Before /(After)** the concert ended, the woman left the building.

    Event 1   Event 2

2. She caught a taxi **when / before** she got outside.

    Event 2   Event 1

3. **Before / After** she told the taxi driver her address, she got in the taxi.

    Event 2   Event 1

4. **Before / When** the taxi stopped, the woman got out of the car.

    Event 1   Event 2

5. **When / Before** the taxi drove away, the woman realized she left her purse in the back seat.

    Event 1   Event 2

6. **Before / After** the taxi driver saw the purse, he opened it.

    Event 1   Event 2

7. He was shocked **before / when** he saw $20,000 in cash.

    Event 2   Event 1

8. The woman got home **before / after** she remembered her purse.

    Event 1   Event 2

9. **Before / After** she called the taxi company, she heard a knock on the door.

    Event 1   Event 2

10. **Before / When** she opened the door, the taxi driver smiled at her.

    Event 1   Event 2

11. He gave the woman the purse **before / after** she hugged him.

    Event 1   Event 2

12. She took out some money **before / after** she opened her purse.

    Event 2   Event 1

13. He thanked the woman **before / when** she gave him $1,000.

    Event 2   Event 1

14. The driver's wife didn't believe him **when / before** he told her the story!

    Event 2   Event 1

3 Combine the sentences below using the time clause words below. Add commas where necessary.

1. The mailman delivered the mail to Sasha's house. Then Sasha returned from work.

   The mailman delivered the mail to Sasha's house before _Sasha returned from work_ .

2. She walked in the door. Then she picked up her mail.

   _____ after _____ .

3. She looked at her mail. Sasha noticed a letter from Vacations Unlimited.

   _____ when _____ .

4. She opened the envelope. Then she read the letter.

   _____ before _____ .

5. She learned that she won a free vacation. She got excited.

   _____ when _____ .

6. The letter asked Sasha to pay a $50 fee. She thought about it.

   When _____ .

7. Sasha sent the $50. Then she waited for a reply.

   After _____ .

8. She waited two weeks for a reply. Then she called the company.

   Before _____ .

9. The company didn't respond to her calls. She knew this was a scam.

   When _____ .

10. She realized she lost her $50. Then she called the police.

    After _____ .

Avoid Common Mistakes

1 Circle the mistakes.

1. (Befor) Jessica got **home, she stopped** for gas.
   (a)   (b)   (c)

2. **After** she wrote **the check she put** it in the mail.
   (a)   (b)   (c)

3. **After** she called the **company, realized** it was a scam.
   (a)   (b)   (c)

4. She **smiled, when she read** the letter.
        (a)   (b)   (c)

5. **He saw** the wallet **afther** the **man got out** of the car.
   (a)   (b)   (c)

6. **When** she arrived **at work she opened** her e-mail.
   (a)   (b)   (c)

7. **Whin** Karina saw her credit card **bill, she realized** someone stole her information.
   (a)   (b)   (c)

8. **She knew** she lost the **money when talked** with the police.
   (a)   (b)   (c)

2 Read the story about an e-mail scam. Find and correct eight more mistakes.

Becky was checking the news online when ^she received an e-mail. The e-mail was from a

man called Adam. Adam said he had gone to the same college as Becky. A few months ago,

Adam started feeling sick. After visited the doctor, the doctor told Adam that he needed

surgery. The surgery was very expensive. Whin Adam learned that he needed surgery he

e-mailed Becky. Adam's e-mail asked Becky to lend him some money.

Afther Becky read this, she tried to remember who Adam was. Becky called her best

friend Dena. Dena also went to college with Becky. After Dena answered her phone,

Becky asked if Dena remembered Adam. When Becky explained about the e-mail, Dena

told her not to send any money. Befor Becky said anything, Dena told her this was a

common scam.

When Becky heard this she was glad she did not mail money to Adam. She deleted the

e-mail, after she hung up. When Becky thought about the scam later that day, realized she

should be more careful in the future.

Self-Assessment

Circle the word or phrase that correctly completes each sentence.

1. _____ he asked her to send money.

   a. When Sandra spoke to   b. Sandra spoke to   c. When spoke to
      the man,   the man,   the man

2. The man charged her credit card (Event 1) _____ Sandra could stop him. (Event 2)

   a. before   b. after   c. when

3. When she realized her mistake, _____ .

   a. when it was too late   b. it was too late   c. before it was too late

4. _____ , the company canceled her credit card.

   a. She called   b. Afther she called   c. After she called

5. She received a new credit card _____ .

   a. before she checked her mail   b. she checked her mail   c. after she checked her mail

6. Robert ate at the restaurant (Event 2) _____ he finished work. (Event 1)

   a. after   b. before   c. afther

7. _____ he bought the ticket.

   a. After he chose the   b. After he chose the   c. After chose the
      numbers,   numbers   numbers

8. He knew he won _____ the numbers on TV.

   a. he saw   b. when saw   c. when he saw

9. _____ Robert heard the good news (Event 1), he got very excited and returned to the restaurant. (Event 2)

   a. When   b. After   c. Before

10. _____ he bought a new car.

    a. After Robert won the money,   b. After won the money   c. After Robert won the money

11. _____ the mailman arrived on Monday (Event 1), Robert received a check. (Event 2)

    a. After   b. Before   c. When

12. When she realized it was a scam, _____ .

    a. after she called the police   b. before she called the police   c. she called the police

13. The taxi driver thanked the woman (Event 2) _____ she gave him $1,000. (Event 1)

    a. before   b. after   c. before,

14. _____ he didn't expect to see $20,000.

    a. He opened the purse,   b. Before opened the purse   c. When he opened the purse,

15. Sasha called _____ $50.

    a. the police, when she lost   b. the police when lost   c. the police when she lost

Count and Noncount Nouns

Eating Habits

Count and Noncount Nouns

1 Read the paragraph below. Decide whether each of the nouns in bold is count or noncount. Write them in the chart below.

Saida shops for her **family** every week. She always buys **milk**, and she gets **chips** and **granola**, too. She also buys **meat**, **seafood**, **tomatoes**, **carrots**, **onions**, **rice**, and **beans** to prepare her **dinners**. For her **lunches**, she gets **bread**, **cheese**, **apples**, and **bananas**. Everyone is happy when she returns with all this **food**.

Count Nouns	Noncount Nouns
family	*milk*

2 Read the conversation. Write *a* or *an* for the count nouns. Write ∅ for the noncount nouns.

Mary: I always eat a big breakfast. I have __*an*__ egg with _____ toast and
(1)   (2)

_____ butter. Then I have _____ cereal. And you?
(3)   (4)

Paul: My breakfast is pretty light. I have _____ apple and _____ bagel. And
(5)   (6)

what do you eat for lunch?

Mary: For lunch, I usually have _____ sandwich and _____ orange!
(7)   (8)

Paul: I often prepare _____ rice with _____ fish, or sometimes I have
(9)   (10)

_____ pasta. I usually add _____ onion, _____ cheese, and
(11)   (12)   (13)

_____ spinach. I love it!
(14)

3 Complete the sentences about the food Nina eats and cooks with. Use the correct form of the verbs in parentheses.

1. Broccoli _*is*_ (be) Nina's favorite food.

2. Blueberries _____ (keep) her brain healthy.

3. Soda _____ (make) her tired.

4. Milk _____ (help) her bones stay strong.

5. Honey _____ (give) her energy.

6. Olive oil _____ (add) flavor to her salads.

7. Nuts and seeds _____ (contain) important nutrients for her.

8. Water _____ (keep) her hydrated.

9. Sugar _____ (affect) her negatively.

10. Oranges _____ (be) her favorite fruit.

11. Spinach _____ (have) iron for her body.

12. Chocolate _____ (make) her happy!

4 Write answers to the questions about the food you eat. Use count and noncount nouns with the correct form of the verbs.

1. **Q:** What do you have for breakfast?   **A:** _I have an egg with toast for breakfast._

2. **Q:** What is your favorite food?   **A:** _____

3. **Q:** What vegetables do you enjoy?   **A:** _____

4. **Q:** What do you like to eat for dinner?   **A:** _____

5. **Q:** What snack food do you like?   **A:** _____

6. **Q:** What kinds of food do you dislike?   **A:** _____

Units of Measure, *How Many . . . ?* and *How Much . . . ?*

1 Complete the conversations. Circle the correct words and write the correct form of the verbs in bold.

1. **Q:** (How much)/ How many fish (do)/ does you

     ___buy___ each week?

   A: I **buy** about five pounds of fish every week.

2. **Q:** How much / How many sandwiches **do / does**

     your son _____ for lunch?

   A: He **eats** two sandwiches for lunch. He has a big appetite.

3. **Q:** How much / How many water **do / does** your

     children _____ every day?

   A: They **drink** eight glasses of water every day.

4. **Q:** How much / How many cups of coffee **do / does** your husband _____

     each morning?

   A: He **drinks** two cups of coffee every morning.

5. **Q:** How much / How many sugar **do / does** he _____ in his coffee?

   A: He doesn't **put** any sugar in his coffee.

6. **Q:** How much / How many eggs **do / does** you _____ in a month?

   A: I **use** about a dozen eggs in a month.

7. **Q:** <u>How much / How many</u> apples **do / does** your daughter _____ every day?

   A: She **eats** one apple a day.

8. **Q:** <u>How much / How many</u> milk **do / does** the children _____ at dinner?

   A: They **drink** two glasses of milk at dinner.

9. **Q:** <u>How much / How many</u> snacks **do / does** the children _____ during the day?

   A: They **eat** two snacks a day.

10. **Q:** <u>How much / How many</u> tea **do / does** you _____ after dinner?

    A: I **make** one pot of tea after dinner.

11. **Q:** <u>How much / How many</u> cans of tuna **do / does** she _____ each week?

    A: She **buys** six cans of tuna each week.

12. **Q:** <u>How much / How many</u> bread **do / does** you _____ in two days?

    A: I **sell** about ten loaves of bread in two days.

13. **Q:** <u>How much / How many</u> boxes of cookies **do / does** the school _____ for

    the party?

    A: The school **orders** six boxes of cookies for the party.

14. **Q:** <u>How much / How many</u> pounds of chicken **do / does** your husband _____ for

    dinner tonight?

    A: My husband **needs** two pounds of chicken for dinner tonight.

15. **Q:** <u>How much / How many</u> dog food **do / does** you _____ in a month?

    A: We **buy** two bags of dog food each month.

2 Look at the picture below. Write questions and answers about Katie's grocery shopping habits with *How many* and *How much*.

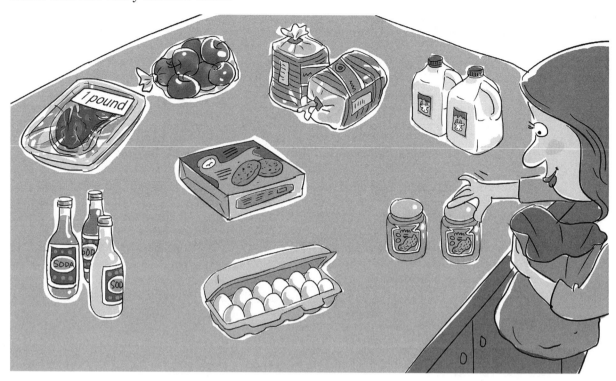

1. **Q:** bread / Katie / have

   A: loaf

   How much bread does Katie have?
   She has two loaves of bread.

2. **Q:** milk / she / buy

   A: gallon

   _____

   _____

3. **Q:** apples / she / get

   A: bag

   _____

   _____

4. **Q:** meat / she / purchase

   A: pound

   _____

   _____

5. **Q:** soda / she / buy

   A: bottle

   _____

   _____

6. **Q:** cookies / she / have

   A: box

   _____

   _____

7. **Q:** eggs / she / get

   A: carton

   _____

   _____

8. **Q:** peanut butter / she / purchase

   A: jar

   _____

   _____

Avoid Common Mistakes

1 Circle the mistakes.

1. To get a good **job**, you must study hard, do all your (**homeworks**) and attend all your **classes**.
   (a)   (b)   (c)
2. In the workforce, health **insurance are** often an important **benefit** of the job.
   (a) (b)   (c)
3. **How much** benefits does a **company** usually offer new **employees**?
   (a)   (b)   (c)
4. In order to make money in **a business**, **a research** into the local **markets** is necessary.
   (a)   (b)   (c)
5. Layla received **information** about the college. **These informations was** helpful.
   (a)   (b)   (c)
6. **How many** furniture does your **office** have for its **employees**?
   (a)   (b)   (c)
7. The TV news **reports** the traffic and **a weather** around the country for business **travelers**.
   (a)   (b)   (c)
8. José bought **software** for his computer. He needed **those softwares** for his **work**.
   (a)   (b)   (c)

2 Find and correct seven more mistakes in the article below.

How to Avoid Sugar

How much
~~How many~~ sugar do you eat? How many protein do you eat? Do you get tired during the workday? Susan tries to eat a healthy diet, but it is not easy because she loves sugars. She knows sugar is not good for her, and it makes her very tired during the day. Instead, she starts her day with protein. For breakfast, she has a milk and two eggs. Sometimes she is still hungry. She wants a donut, but she tries to resist. For a morning snack, she has a cheese and waters. She prefers cookies, but she knows that when she eats them, the sugar makes her tired about an hour later. She eats soup and vegetables for lunch. These soups are part of her healthy diet. Susan avoids high sugar intake during the day, but after dinner, she finally has a small, sweet dessert. After a long day, she deserves a break! She ends her day with a cup of tea or a small glass of milks.

Self-Assessment

Circle the word or phrase that correctly completes each sentence.

1. Researchers say that _____ a good source of calcium.

    a. milk is   b. milks is   c. milk are

2. Tania's sandwich had _____ and some turkey.

    a. cheeses   b. a cheese   c. a piece of cheese

3. It can be _____ for many people to stay on a healthy diet.

    a. challenge   b. a challenge   c. challenges

4. _____ do you drink in the morning?

    a. How many coffee   b. How much coffee   c. How much coffees

5. The school's new _____ very expensive.

    a. equipment was   b. equipment were   c. equipments were

6. Information about good food _____ me eat better.

    a. help   b. helps   c. is help

7. _____ do restaurant chefs receive on preparing healthy food?

    a. How much trainings   b. How many trainings   c. How much training

8. Sometimes the TV news _____ on eating habits in the United States.

    a. reports   b. report   c. is reports

9. Chris has _____ in his salad every day.

    a. spinaches   b. spinach   c. a spinach

10. Every afternoon, I drink _____ .

    a. cup of teas   b. cup of tea   c. a cup of tea

11. _____ do psychologists do on eating habits?

    a. How much researches   b. How many research   c. How much research

12. Diane is allergic to _____ .

    a. seafoods   b. a seafood   c. seafood

13. I think _____ is very comfortable.

    a. those furnitures   b. that furniture   c. a furniture

14. The _____ how I feel.

    a. weathers affect   b. weather affect   c. weather affects

15. Do you drink _____ every day?

    a. a glasses of juice   b. a glass of juices   c. a glass of juice

Quantifiers: *Some, Any, A Lot Of, A Little, A Few, Much, Many*

Languages

Quantifiers: *Some* and *Any*

1 Complete the e-mail to students from the college language lab coordinator. Circle the correct quantifiers.

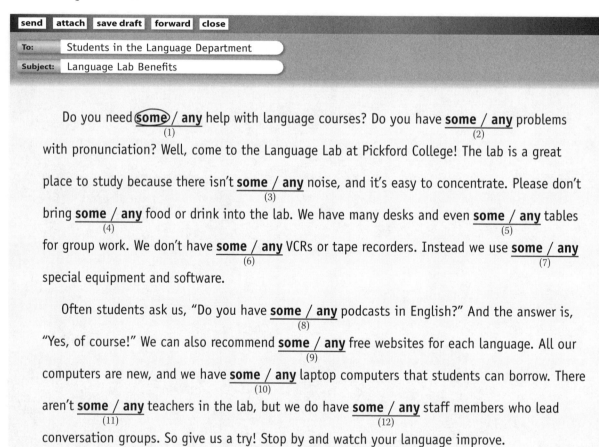

send | attach | save draft | forward | close

To: Students in the Language Department

Subject: Language Lab Benefits

Do you need **some** / any help with language courses? Do you have **some / any** problems
(1)   (2)
with pronunciation? Well, come to the Language Lab at Pickford College! The lab is a great

place to study because there isn't **some / any** noise, and it's easy to concentrate. Please don't
(3)
bring **some / any** food or drink into the lab. We have many desks and even **some / any** tables
(4)   (5)
for group work. We don't have **some / any** VCRs or tape recorders. Instead we use **some / any**
(6)   (7)
special equipment and software.

Often students ask us, "Do you have **some / any** podcasts in English?" And the answer is,
(8)
"Yes, of course!" We can also recommend **some / any** free websites for each language. All our
(9)
computers are new, and we have **some / any** laptop computers that students can borrow. There
(10)
aren't **some / any** teachers in the lab, but we do have **some / any** staff members who lead
(11)   (12)
conversation groups. So give us a try! Stop by and watch your language improve.

2 Olga, Sam, and Carlos are talking about their strategies for learning a language. Use the information in the chart to write sentences with *some* and *any* about the strategies. Note that ✓ = *some* and ✗ = *not any*.

	Olga	Carlos	Sam
Have English songs on the computer	✓	✗	✓
Watch TV shows in English	✓	✓	✗
Read news online in English	✗	✓	✓
Speak English outside of class	✓	✓	✗
Read books in English	✗	✓	✗
Write e-mails in English	✓	✗	✓

1. Olga / have English songs on the computer

    Olga has some English songs on the computer.

2. Carlos / have English songs on the computer

    Carlos doesn't have any English songs on the computer.

3. Sam / watch TV shows in English

    _____

4. Sam and Carlos / read news online in English

    _____

5. Sam / speak English outside of class

    _____

6. Olga and Sam / read books in English

    _____

7. Carlos / read books in English

    _____

8. Carlos / write e-mails in English

    _____

9. Sam / write e-mails in English

    _____

3 Complete the questions and answers. Use *some* or *any* and the words in parentheses.

1. **Q:** (Are there / languages that no longer exist) _Are there any languages that no longer exist?_

    A: Yes, _there are some languages that no longer exist_ .

2. **Q:** (Does / English / use / accent marks) _____

    _____

    A: No, _____ .

3. **Q:** (Are there / English words in other languages) _____

    _____

    A: Yes, _____ .

4. **Q:** (Does / our college / offer / classes in Portuguese) _____

    _____

    A: Yes, _____ .

5. **Q:** (Are there / articles in the Russian language) _____

    _____

    A: No, _____ .

6. **Q:** (Are there / websites for learning Polish) _____

    _____

    A: Yes, _____ .

7. **Q:** (Does / Chinese / have / past forms of verbs) _____

    _____

    A: No, _____ .

8. **Q:** (Do / other languages / have / special past forms for literature) _____

    _____

    A: Yes, _____ .

Quantifiers: *A Lot Of, A Little, A Few, Much, Many*

1 Complete the student blog. Circle the correct quantifiers.

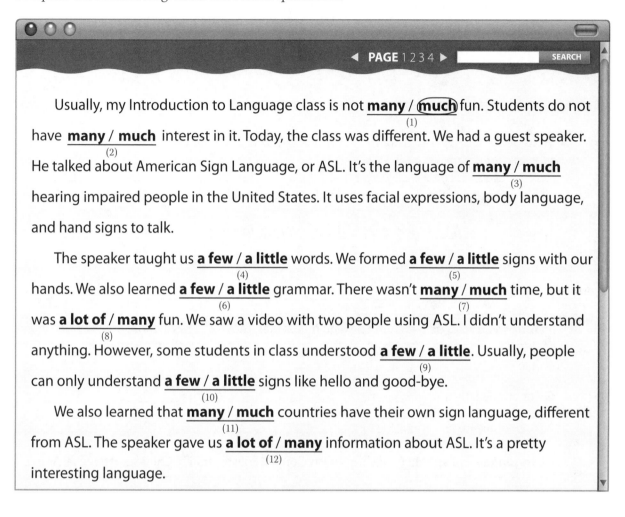

Usually, my Introduction to Language class is not **many / (much)** fun. Students do not
(1)

have **many / much** interest in it. Today, the class was different. We had a guest speaker.
(2)

He talked about American Sign Language, or ASL. It's the language of **many / much**
(3)

hearing impaired people in the United States. It uses facial expressions, body language,

and hand signs to talk.

The speaker taught us **a few / a little** words. We formed **a few / a little** signs with our
(4) (5)

hands. We also learned **a few / a little** grammar. There wasn't **many / much** time, but it
(6) (7)

was **a lot of / many** fun. We saw a video with two people using ASL. I didn't understand
(8)

anything. However, some students in class understood **a few / a little**. Usually, people
(9)

can only understand **a few / a little** signs like hello and good-bye.
(10)

We also learned that **many / much** countries have their own sign language, different
(11)

from ASL. The speaker gave us **a lot of / many** information about ASL. It's a pretty
(12)

interesting language.

2 Write sentences with the information below. Choose the correct quantifiers.

1. The language department in my college / offer / different languages – (many / much)

   The language department in my college offers many different languages.

2. It / have / technology – (much / a lot of)

   _____

3. There not be / listening practice / in the Latin classes – (many / much)

   _____

4. The language teachers / give / homework – (many / a lot of)

   _____

5. The language lab / provide / DVD players – (a few / a little)

   _____

6. The English students / practice / pronunciation – (a few / a little)

_____

7. There not be / translation practice – (many / much)

_____

8. There be / French teachers in the language department – (much / many)

_____

3 Write sentences with some of the nouns in the box or use your own nouns. Use *a lot of, much, a little, many,* or *a few.*

| **Things your English teacher uses in class:** markers, chalk, paper, music, books, MP3s, websites |

1. a little   _My teacher uses a little music in class._____

2. a lot of   _____

3. a few   _____

| **Things you read or watch in English:** magazines, movies, news, fiction, novels, poetry |

4. a few   _____

5. much (negative)   _____

6. many (negative)   _____

| **Languages you speak:** English, Spanish, Somali, Polish, French, Chinese, Japanese, Arabic |

7. a little   _____

8. much (negative)   _____

4 Write questions with *a lot of, much, a little, many,* or *a few.* Then give answers that are true for you.

1. many / your teacher / show / movies in class

   Q: _Does your teacher show many movies in class?_____

   A: _No, she doesn't show many movies._____

2. much / there be / noise / in your neighborhood

   Q: _____

   A: _____

3. a lot of / your friends / send / text messages

Q: _____

A: _____

4. a few / you / have / books in English

Q: _____

A: _____

Avoid Common Mistakes

1 Circle the mistakes.

1. (Much) words in **English** come from other languages. Do you know **any**?
   (a)   (b)   (c)

2. **Some** dictionaries don't have **many** information about **loanwords**.
   (a)   (b)   (c)

3. I don't know **some** loanwords from **Korean** in other languages. Are there **any**?
                (a)   (b)   (c)

4. I did **a research** on **some** loanwords from French, and English has **many**.
        (a)   (b)   (c)

5. I write **much** e-mails to **many** people. **Some** of my e-mails are in different languages.
           (a)   (b)   (c)

6. My sister has **a contact** with **many** Canadians, but I don't have **any**.
                (a)   (b)   (c)

7. **Some** teachers don't give **some** homework because the students don't have **any** time to do it.
   (a)   (b)   (c)

8. **Many** Americans don't have **many** knowledge about the **many** languages in Africa.
   (a)   (b)   (c)

2 Find and correct seven more mistakes from Professor Soto's Spanish class website.

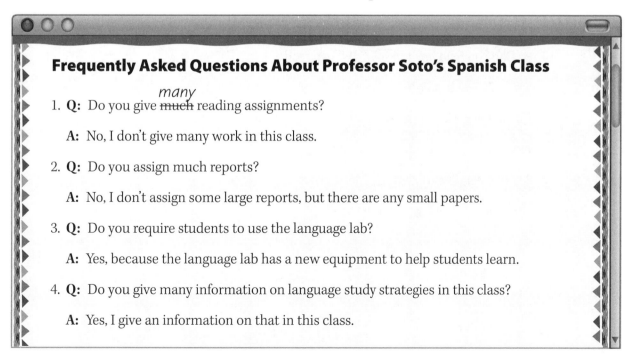

Frequently Asked Questions About Professor Soto's Spanish Class

1. **Q:** Do you give ~~much~~ *many* reading assignments?

   A: No, I don't give many work in this class.

2. **Q:** Do you assign much reports?

   A: No, I don't assign some large reports, but there are any small papers.

3. **Q:** Do you require students to use the language lab?

   A: Yes, because the language lab has a new equipment to help students learn.

4. **Q:** Do you give many information on language study strategies in this class?

   A: Yes, I give an information on that in this class.

Self-Assessment

Circle the word or phrase that correctly completes each sentence.

1. My parents don't have _____ contact with languages other than English.

   a. much   b. many   c. some

2. My neighbors taught me _____ in American Sign Language.

   a. a little words   b. a few words   c. much

3. There are _____ signs in American Sign Language that use the face.

   a. many   b. any   c. much

4. Do you know _____ signs in American Sign Language?

   a. any   b. a little   c. much

5. There aren't _____ students from Madagascar in my English program.

   a. some   b. any   c. a little

6. There are _____ students from Mali in my French class.

   a. a little   b. much   c. a few

7. English imports words from _____ languages.

   a. much   b. a lot of   c. a little

8. I did _____ research on the words that English exports to other languages.

   a. a   b. some   c. much

9. Did you learn _____ Spanish on your trip to the Dominican Republic?

   a. many   b. a few   c. any

10. **A:** Can you read any Russian? **B:** I can read _____ .

    a. much   b. a little   c. a few

11. The language lab at my school has _____ computers.

    a. a little   b. much   c. many

12. My teacher doesn't give _____ homework.

    a. some   b. a few   c. a lot of

13. Does your language lab have _____ special equipment for students?

    a. many   b. a   c. any

14. My teacher doesn't know _____ students from Morocco.

    a. some   b. much   c. any

15. It is important to have _____ contact with other languages and cultures.

    a. a   b. some   c. many

Articles: *A / An* and *The*

Changes and Risks

Articles: *A / An* and *The*

1 Read the story about a risk a woman named Sandra took. Circle the correct articles.

Two years ago, Sandra made **a**/**an** big decision that changed her life. Sandra
(1)

worked as **the**/**a** waitress for 15 years. One day, she heard **a**/**an** advertisement on **an**/**the**
(2)   (3)   (4)

radio. It was about **a**/**an** exciting new career as **a**/**an** emergency medical technician. She
(5)   (6)

lived near **a**/**an** community college. **A**/**The** college offered classes in emergency medical
(7)   (8)

technology. She took **a**/**an** anatomy class. After she started **a**/**the** college's class, she liked
(9)   (10)

it. She quit her job and took more classes. She finished **an**/**the** program and applied for
(11)

a/**the** job. **A**/**The** job was as at **a**/**an** hospital near her house. **An**/**The** hospital called her
(12)   (13)   (14)   (15)

in for **an**/**the** interview. Now she works at **a**/**the** hospital and she is happy she decided to
(16)   (17)

take a risk and change careers.

2 Complete the paragraphs with *a*, *an*, or *the*.

Lucas and his family moved from New York to California. It was __*a*__ big change. They bought
_____ old house near _____ new school.
(2)   (3)
Lucas and his wife read about _____ new school
(4)
on _____ Internet. _____ school website
(5)   (6)
said that _____ school was very good. The
(7)
children started and liked it. They were in _____
(8)
new classroom with _____ excellent teacher.
(9)

In _____ classroom, there was _____ computer for each child. _____ teacher
(10)   (11)   (12)
also had _____ computer. _____ children liked learning on _____ computer.
(13)   (14)   (15)
They also studied in _____ school library in _____ afternoon. Lucas and his wife felt
(16)   (17)
good about _____ decision they made. It was _____ good choice.
(18)   (19)

3 Complete the sentences with *a*, *an*, or *the* and the words in parentheses.

Kyle needed __*a car*__ for work. He wanted _____ (used car), but he
(1)   (2)
knew it could be risky. He found _____ (inexpensive car), but
(3)
_____ (car) had some unusual problems. It did not go fast, its front door had
(4)
_____ (scratch), _____ (sun) had faded _____ (red
(5)   (6)   (7)
paint) to pink, and _____ (radio) didn't work.
(8)

Kyle still wanted _____ (car), so he got _____ (small loan) to
(9)   (10)
buy it. _____ (loan) was very good, and he bought _____ (used car).
(11)   (12)
He drove it to work every day with no problems, but his friends hated it!

4 Greg's life changed from 2005 to today. Write sentences about Greg's life in 2005 and his life today. Use *a*, *an*, or *the* and the words given.

Things Greg Did in 2005

1. Greg / study at / local college

   Greg studied at a local college.

2. He / not use / smartphone

   _____

3. He / work outside in / sun

   _____

4. He / drive / old car

   _____

Things Greg Does Today

5. Greg / teach at / University of Clarkson

   Greg teaches at the University of Clarkson.

6. He / use / smartphone

   _____

7. He / work inside / office

   _____

8. He / drive / new car

   _____

Article or No Article?

1 Complete the sentences with *the* or Ø for no article.

Kim: Eric, I hear you like to take __Ø__ risks. Someone
      (1)

told me you took a big one two years ago. What

did you do?

Eric: Well, when I finished college, I had _____
                                              (2)

job offers from _____ big companies. My
                    (3)

major was _____ English, and I wasn't
             (4)

ready to start _____ work at a company. I
                 (5)

heard about a job teaching _____ English in
                              (6)

_____ Spain. _____ job didn't pay much
   (7)   (8)

money, but I wanted to get _____ experience teaching overseas. I responded
                             (9)

to _____ companies and said no. Then I went to _____ Europe to teach
     (10)   (11)

English for one year.

Kim: Where did you go when you were there?

Eric: I lived and taught in Barcelona, but I had a lot of free time to travel, too. I saw a lot

of _____ different places on vacation. I saw _____ Pyrenees and _____
     (12)   (13)   (14)

Alps, the two most famous mountain ranges in _____ Europe. I visited
(15)

_____ Mont Blanc in France. It is the highest mountain in western Europe. I saw
(16)

_____ Eiffel Tower. I also took a boat ride along _____ Thames, a famous
(17)   (18)

river in _____ England. I met a lot of great people in my job and during
(19)

my travels.

Kim: Wow! And now you have a job with me in _____ Chrysler Building in New York.
(20)

Eric: That's right. I'm not afraid of taking _____ risks.
(21)

2 Complete the sentences. Write the words in parentheses with *the* or no article.

Mary doesn't usually like to take her children to __*restaurants*__ (restaurants). She
(1)

likes to prepare _____ (food) at _____ (home). She likes to cook,
(2)   (3)

especially when she has _____ (guests).
(4)

Last week, a new restaurant opened near her _____ (house). Her friend
(5)

gave her _____ (address) of this new place. It was a seafood restaurant.
(6)

Her children love _____ (seafood). So, Mary took a risk and hoped
(7)

_____ (food) was good. They went to _____ (restaurant) and
(8)   (9)

looked at _____ (menu). It all looked wonderful on the menu.
(10)

When they got _____ (food), it was cold, and _____ (waiters)
(11)   (12)

were not friendly. Mary was not happy. She took _____ (children) to a
(13)

movie theater. In _____ (movie theater), they bought
(14)

_____ (hot dogs) with _____ (onions). Finally, her children
(15)   (16)

were happy.

3 Use the map to complete the sentences about places in North America. Use *the* or no article.

1. _____*The Beaufort Sea*_____

   (Beaufort Sea) is a large sea above

   _____*North America*_____ (continent).

2. _____

   (Greenland) is an icy country next to

   _____ (country).

3. _____

   (Mississippi River) is a long river in

   _____ (country).

4. _____

   (Mojave Desert) is a hot desert in

   _____ (country).

5. _____

   (Sierra Madre de Oaxaca)

   is a big mountain range in

   _____ (country).

6. _____ (Mount Whitney) is a tall mountain in

   _____ (country).

7. _____ (Great Lakes) are enormous lakes in

   _____ (two countries).

8. _____ (Rio Grande) is a long river in

   _____ (continent).

North America

ARCTIC OCEAN

Greenland (Denmark)

Beaufort Sea

Canada

Great Lakes

PACIFIC OCEAN

The United States

Mount Whitney
Mojave Desert

Rio Grande

Mississippi River

ATLANTIC OCEAN

Mexico

Sierra Madre de Oaxaca

4 Write questions and answers using *the* or no article before the nouns.

1. **Q:** Where / Nile River   **A:** Africa

   <u>*Where is the Nile River?*</u>   <u>*It is in Africa.*</u>

2. **Q:** Where / Empire State Building   **A:** New York City

   _____   _____

3. **Q:** Where / Grand Canyon   **A:** Arizona

   _____   _____

4. **Q:** Where / Himalayas   **A:** Asia

   _____   _____

5. **Q:** Where / Great Lakes   **A:** Midwest

   _____   _____

6. **Q:** Where / Lake Titicaca   **A:** Peru and Bolivia

   _____   _____

7. **Q:** Where / Mount McKinley   **A:** Alaska

   _____   _____

8. **Q:** Where / Great Plains   **A:** United States and Canada

   _____   _____

Avoid Common Mistakes

1 Circle the mistakes.

1. Francesco found **information** in (**on the Italy**) to help him with his **report**.
   (a)   (b)   (c)

2. When Cathy was **a girl** in **high school**, she often took **the risks**.
   (a)   (b)   (c)

3. I purchased **books** about **the United Arab Emirates** before I moved there for
   (a)   (b)

   an new job.
   (c)

4. Rock climbers take **risks**. They don't worry about **a money** or **a stable job**.
   (a)   (b)   (c)

5. **Some people** need **a security** more than they need **adventure**.
   (a)   (b)   (c)

6. Maria doesn't like her **job**. She wants to enjoy **the life** and see **the world**.
   (a)   (b)   (c)

7. **People** lose **jobs** in **an bad economy**.
   (a)   (b)   (c)

8. Marcos left his **job** to teach **English** in **the Europe**.
   (a)   (b)   (c)

2 Find and correct eight more mistakes in this article.

Taking a Risk

When the economy is bad, ~~the~~ people can lose jobs. The life becomes more difficult. Money can be an problem. Gary Hawke knows this personally. He had a stable job in the Australia. He had a health insurance, a good boss, and friendly co-workers. However, his company closed, and he lost his job. Many people in his country lost their jobs because companies closed. Gary took a big risk and moved to the Canada. He heard they had jobs. At first, he had a trouble finding a job. Finally, he found work at a Internet research company. Now, he loves his new job and new friends. Big problems sometimes require taking the big risks.

Self-Assessment

Circle the word or phrase that correctly completes each sentence.

1. Robert went to _____ university in England to study business.

    a. an   b. a   c. big

2. Lorena needed _____ to make a good decision.

    a. a time   b. an time   c. time

3. Everyone talks about _____ these days.

    a. economy   b. the economy   c. an economy

4. Bill took a risk and bought a car. _____ was very expensive.

    a. The car   b. A car   c. Car

5. Alex and Marie took a risk and bought their son _____ .

    a. a unusual gift   b. unusual gift   c. an unusual gift

6. Some people want everything in _____ to be stable.

    a. life   b. the life   c. a life

7. There are _____ when you start a new business.

    a. a risks   b. the risks   c. risks

8. Marina's family moved from _____ to the United States last year.

   a. the Russia   b. Russia   c. a Russia

9. Some colleges assign _____ to international students.

   a. language tutors   b. a language tutors   c. language tutor

10. Susan had a problem. She took a risk and fixed _____ .

    a. a problem   b. the problem   c. problems

11. Many jobs offer _____ .

    a. a good health insurance   b. good health insurance   c. the good health insurance

12. Peter was an analyst in _____ .

    a. the Asia   b. an Asia   c. Asia

13. I received _____ from my family when I took a risk.

    a. support   b. the support   c. a support

14. Kala took a new job today. It was _____ .

    a. a easy decision   b. an easy decision   c. easy decision

15. People don't often swim in certain parts of _____ . It's too dangerous.

    a. a Colorado River   b. Colorado River   c. the Colorado River

Possessive Pronouns

1 Complete the chart with the possessive pronouns.

Possessive Determiners	Possessive Pronouns
my	1. *mine*
your	2.
his	3.
her	4.
its	5.
our	6.
their	7.

2 Read the conversation and circle the correct possessive determiner or possessive pronoun.

Dora: I love the end-of-the-semester potlucks at our school.

Hector: Yeah, they're great. **Ours / Our** classmates bring typical dishes from **their / theirs** home
(1)   (2)
countries. Did you bring one from **yours / your**?
(3)

Dora: Yes, I brought one from **my / mine**. It's called *goulash*, a traditional dish
$\underset{(4)}{}$

in Hungary. People in **mine / my** home country love it.
$\underset{(5)}{}$

Hector: Put it here on the table next to Martina's dish.

Dora: What's **her / hers** dish?
$\underset{(6)}{}$

Hector: **Hers / Her** is *pupusas*. Pupusas are a traditional dish from El Salvador.
$\underset{(7)}{}$

Dora: What's that table over there with more food?

Hector: That's from the students in the morning class. **Theirs / Their** table also has many
$\underset{(8)}{}$

traditional dishes from their home countries.

Dora: I think **our / ours** has more food than **theirs / their**.
$\underset{(9)}{}$ $\underset{(10)}{}$

Hector: Well, all the students from that class aren't here yet. **Theirs / Their** is filling
$\underset{(11)}{}$

up quickly.

3 Complete the paragraphs with possessive pronouns *mine, yours, his, hers, ours,* or *theirs.*

Wanda, her roommates, and their neighbor all shop at different stores. Wanda buys her food

at the Mercado. Her roommates get _*theirs*_ at Plus Market. Wanda buys _____ separately
$\underset{(1)}{}$ $\underset{(2)}{}$

because she has a different diet. Their neighbor Bill shops for _____ at Shopmart. The girls
$\underset{(3)}{}$

usually do their shopping on Fridays, and Bill does _____ on Saturdays.
$\underset{(4)}{}$

My roommate Joe and I buy our groceries at Big Food. The girls' food is very expensive, but

_____ is not expensive because we shop at an inexpensive store. The food we buy is always
$\underset{(5)}{}$

on sale, but the girls don't buy _____ on sale. They don't use coupons to buy their food, but
$\underset{(6)}{}$

we use coupons for _____ . Joe and I share a lot of our food, but I have a few things that are
$\underset{(7)}{}$

_____ . He has a few things that are _____ . Sometimes he doesn't remember which items
$\underset{(8)}{}$ $\underset{(9)}{}$

belong to me. He asks me, "Is this _____ ?" And I say, "Yes, it's mine!" It's usually a good system.
$\underset{(10)}{}$

4 Complete each question with *mine, yours, his, hers, ours,* or *theirs.* Then write the answer
with the words in parentheses and the correct possessive pronoun.

1. **Q:** We drink our tea in the morning. When do **you** drink _*yours*_ ?

   A: (we / drink / at night) _*We drink ours at night.*_____

2. **Q:** I put milk in my coffee. What do **you** put in _____ ?

   A: (I / put / sugar in) _____

3. **Q:** Vicki likes her eggs soft. How do **Janet and Joe** like _____ ?

   A: (they / like / soft) _____

4. **Q:** Rick puts his vitamins in the refrigerator. Where does **John** put _____ ?

   A: (he / put / in the cabinet) _____

5. **Q:** Sofia uses her big pan for rice. What does **Mary** use _____ for?

   A: (she / use / for noodles) _____

6. **Q:** I buy my fruit at the farmers' market. Where do **you** buy _____ ?

   A: (I / buy / at the supermarket) _____

7. **Q:** We have our class potluck tomorrow. When do **you** have _____ ?

   A: (we / have / on Friday) _____

8. **Q:** My children eat their snack at 2:00 p.m. When do **your children** eat _____ ?

   A: (they / eat / at 4:00 p.m.) _____

Indefinite Pronouns

1 Complete the conversation with -one, -body, or -thing. Sometimes there is more than one correct answer.

Jin-ju: Thanks for a great party, Hiro.

Hiro: No problem. It was fun. But it's quiet now.

Jin-ju: Is any_one_ OR _body_ still here?
            (1)

Hiro: No, I think every_____ left.
               (2)

Jin-ju: Did any_____ stay and help you clean up?
          (3)

Hiro: No, no_____ stayed and helped.
          (4)

Jin-ju: Well, I can help you.

Hiro: OK. Let's clean all the tables. First, we can take

    every_____ off of them.
         (5)

Jin-ju: Is there any_____ else I can do?
         (6)

Hiro: Well, some_____ always leaves a purse or
         (7)

    cell phone. Jeff probably did that. He's so forgetful! Also, I think Lana left

    some_____ on the chair over there. Is that her purse?
        (8)

Jin-ju: No, it's *no_____ . It's just an empty box.
(9)

  Hiro: Do you want to listen to any particular music as we clean?

Jin-ju: No, *any_____ is fine with me. Play whatever you like.
(10)

  Hiro: Great! I want to finish this quickly. I'm so tired . . . I just want some sleep!

2 Complete the sentences about traditional Japanese restaurants. Circle the correct indefinite pronouns.

In Japan, an expensive, traditional restaurant treats you well. After you enter the

restaurant, **anyone / (someone)** takes your coat. Then, **everyone / anyone** removes their
(1)   (2)

shoes. Next, you sit on a cushion on the floor at a small table.

Everyone / No one sits in a chair. After that, **someone / anyone**
(3)   (4)

in traditional Japanese dress serves you. You do not receive

a menu. The food is already prepared, so you don't order

nothing / anything. **Everybody / Anybody** usually eats with
(5)   (6)

chopsticks, but **anyone / no one** who needs a fork can ask for
(7)

one. When you need **nothing / something**, your server is always
(8)

there to help you. **Everything / Anything** is always delicious.
(9)

Nothing / Anything is left on the plate. **Everybody / Anybody**
(10)   (11)

always enjoys a nice evening at this type of restaurant.

3 Use the picture to answer the questions. Use the words in parentheses and indefinite pronouns from the box.

anybody	anything	everyone	nothing
anyone	~~everyone~~	no one	something

1. **Q:** Is **anyone** around the table?

   A: Yes, _everyone is around the table_ _____ (is / around the table).

2. **Q:** Do you see **anybody** next to the refrigerator

   A: No, _____ (I / don't see / next to the refrigerator).

3. **Q:** Is there **anything** on the counter?

   A: No, _____ (there / is / on the counter).

4. **Q:** Does **anyone** have food on their plates?

   A: Yes, _____ (has / food on their plates).

5. **Q:** Is there **anything** on the stove?

   A: Yes, _____ (there / is / on the stove).

6. **Q:** Is there **anything** over the table?

   A: No, _____ (there / isn't / over the table).

7. **Q:** Is **anybody** next to the stove?

   A: No, _____ (is / next to the stove).

8. **Q:** Do you see **anyone** on the phone?

   A: No, _____ (there / isn't / on the phone).

Avoid Common Mistakes

1 Circle the mistakes.

1. **Jessica's breakfast** is small, and (mine breakfast) is big. How's **your breakfast**?

(a)   (b)   (c)

2. I don't eat **nothing** for breakfast. She has **nothing** for breakfast. Do you have **anything**

(a)   (b)   (c)

for breakfast?

3. These eggs are **yours**. Those eggs are **mines**, and **his** are still on the stove.

               (a)   (b)   (c)

4. I brought **my** dish to the potluck, and they brought **there's**. Did you bring **yours**?

         (a)   (b)   (c)

5. **Her** coffee is cold, and **mine** is cold, too. Why is **yours coffee** still hot?

  (a)   (b)   (c)

6. Those vitamins are **his**. **Mines** are on the top shelf, and **yours** are on the bottom.

                (a)   (b)   (c)

7. Jane saw **someone** she knew at the party. I saw **somebody** I knew, but Bob didn't see **nobody**.

           (a)   (b)   (c)

8. **His** food is always good. **There's** is tasty, but **mine** is the best.

  (a)   (b)   (c)

2 Find and correct seven more mistakes from Francesca's e-mail to her mother.

| send | attach | save draft | forward | close |

From: Francesca <francesca45@cambridge.org>

To: Mom <mom11@cambridge.org>

Subject: Dinner Last Night

Hi Mom,

    I went to Aunt Lina's house in Brooklyn for dinner last night. It was so interesting. Her family's foods are different from ours ~~foods~~ in Italy. A lot of there's come from cans and boxes. Last night, we had spaghetti and meatballs for dinner. It was good, but she prepared her meatballs differently from the way I prepare mines for my family. I don't think hers meatballs were very fresh. After dinner, we had chocolate cake for dessert. It was good, but they said there's was from a box. I always make mine desserts, and I use all natural ingredients. Mines are never from a box. It was a nice evening. There wasn't nothing wrong with the meal. It was just different.

    Hope to chat soon!

Francesca

Self-Assessment

Circle the word or phrase that correctly completes each sentence.

1. Maria prepared a traditional dish from her home country. Did you bring one from _____ ?

   a. yours   b. yours country   c. your

2. Those tortillas _____ .

   a is her   b. are hers   c. are her

3. After the guests ate, there wasn't _____ left on their plates.

   a. anything   b. nothing   c. anyone

4. A lot of people in Spain eat _____ late at night.

   a. theirs dinners   b. their dinners   c. their

5. Your noodles are delicious. _____ aren't very good.

   a. Hers   b. Hers noodles   c. Ours noodles

6. Did _____ bring tamales to the party?

   a. anything   b. anyone   c. nobody

7. Rita didn't bring _____ to the potluck.

   a. nothing   b. no one   c. anything

8. My dessert was not very good. _____ was delicious.

   a. Theirs dessert   b. There's   c. Theirs

9. Did _____ teach you to cook?

   a. everything   b. anything   c. someone

10. I like dumplings. Do you make _____ with meat or vegetables?

    a. your   b. yours dumplings   c. yours

11. I'd like to know _____ about physical health.

    a. anything   b. something   c. everyone

12. My lunch is usually light, but _____ is a really big meal.

    a. theirs   b. there's   c. theirs lunch

13. _____ in my family loves pizza for dinner.

     a. Anyone   b. Everyone   c. Something

14. Tim's kitchen is always clean. _____ is usually a mess.

     a. Mine kitchen   b. Mine   c. My

15. Those cookies are _____ .

     a. yours   b. yours cookies   c. your

Imperatives

Social Customs

Imperatives

1 Two students are comparing the social customs in South Korea and Venezuela. Complete the sentences with the imperative form of the verbs from the box.

South Korea

be	bow	eat	look	look	~~shake~~	stare

Don't shake (not) hands. Instead, _____ . _____ (not).
    (1)   (2)   (3)

_____ at them and then _____ away. _____
    (4)   (5)   (6)

on time, even for parties. _____ (not) in public.
                                  (7)

Venezuela

be	dance	worry	come	smile

_____ and _____ friendly. _____ (not)
    (8)   (9)   (10)

about time. _____ a half hour or an hour late. Always _____
                (11)   (12)

at the parties you go to.

2 Look at the pictures. Write affirmative or negative imperatives under each sign about the university library rules.

be	eat	enter	listen	~~run~~	show	~~turn off~~	use	wait

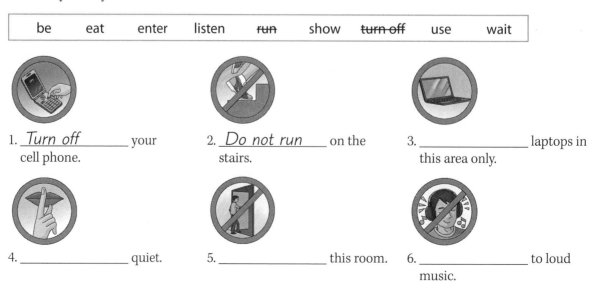

1. _Turn off_____ your cell phone.

2. _Do not run_____ on the stairs.

3. _____ laptops in this area only.

4. _____ quiet.

5. _____ this room.

6. _____ to loud music.

7. _____ in line here.

8. _____ your ID card.

9. _____ in the library

3 A Look at the map. Complete the directions to the different cultural centers in the city. Begin at the *Start* point on the map.

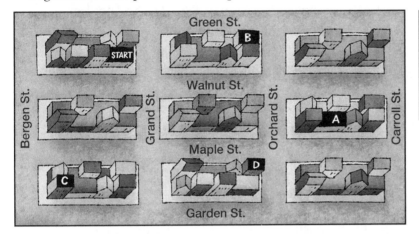

KEY
Start = 32 Walnut Street
A = Asian Cultural Center
B = North African Society
C = Caribbean House
D = Italian-American Association

1. **Wei:** How do I get to the Asian Cultural Center from 32 Walnut Street?

   Juan: Go straight on Walnut Street. Then *turn right* on Orchard Street. Then
   (1)

   _____ on Maple Street. It's on the left.
   (2)

2. **Fatma:** How do I get to the North African Society from 32 Walnut Street?

   Sophie: _____ on Walnut Street. Then _____ onto Orchard
   (3)   (4)

   Street. It's on the corner of Orchard Street and Green Street.

3. **Martine:** How do I get to the Caribbean House from 32 Walnut Street?

   Diego: From Walnut Street, _____ onto Grand Street. Then
   (5)

   _____ on Maple Street. Then _____ onto Bergen
   (6)   (7)

   Street. It's on the corner of Bergen Street and Garden Street.

B Now give Francesco directions to the Italian-American Association.

Francesco: How do I get to the Italian-American Association from 32 Walnut Street?

Go straight on Walnut Street. _____

_____

_____

_____

Avoid Common Mistakes

1 Circle the mistakes.

1. At school, (no be) late, **don't forget** your homework, and **don't eat** in class.
   (a)   (b)   (c)

2. At work, **don't make** personal calls, **donot interrupt** busy people, and **don't wear**
   (a)   (b)   (c)
   short pants.

3. At the pool, **don't bring** glass bottles, **don't splash** water, and **do'nt swim** with
   (a)   (b)   (c)
   shoes on.

4. At the library, **dont chew** gum, **don't talk** loudly, and **don't write** on the desks.
   (a)   (b)   (c)

5. On public transportation, **don't touch** people, **no talk loudly**, and **don't use** two seats.
   (a)   (b)   (c)

6. In the chemistry lab, **don't wear** sandals, **do n't mix** the wrong chemicals, and **don't eat**.
   (a)   (b)   (c)

7. At a nice restaurant, **don't make** cell phone calls, **do n't smoke**, and **don't pay** with
   (a)   (b)   (c)
   a check.

8. In a new culture, **don't stare**, **no shout** when you talk, and **don't point** at people.
   (a)   (b)   (c)

2 Find and correct seven more mistakes in this blog about unspoken rules in a movie theater.

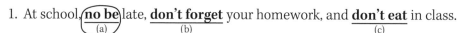

Movie Theater Website   Movie Times · Popular Movies · Trailers · Reviews

Rules to Remember at the Movie Theater

Do not
1. ~~Donot~~ bring babies to the movies.
2. Dont sing along with the music.
3. Do'nt talk during the movie.
4. Donot stand up.

5. No use cell phones.
6. Do n't throw trash on the floor.
7. No put your feet on the chair in front of you.
8. D'ont be late to the movie.

Self-Assessment

Circle the word or phrase that correctly completes each sentence.

1. _____ problems at your job.

   a. Don't cause   b. Don't causes   c. Donot cause

2. Be friendly and _____ to others on your first day of work.

  a. dont listen   b. listens   c. listen

3. _____ down when people talk with you.

  a. Do'nt look   b. Do n't look   c. Don't look

4. _____ attention during meetings at work.

  a. Pays   b. Pay   c. Paid

5. _____ until you know people. Then you can ask about their families.

  a. Wait   b. Dont wait   c. Waited

6. _____ left at the corner.

  a. Do'nt turn   b. No turn   c. Don't turn

7. Walk two blocks and _____ a right.

  a. takes   b. took   c. take

8. _____ the street and enter the building.

  a. Cross   b. No Cross   c. Crosses

9. _____ careful and watch for cars.

  a. Is   b. Are   c. Be

10. _____ straight. Turn right at the corner.

  a. No go   b. Don't go   c. Goes

11. Take care and _____ a nice day.

  a. having   b. has   c. have

12. _____ to turn off the computer before you leave.

  a. Donot forget   b. Dont forget   c. Don't forget

13. _____ a thank-you note to the family for the dinner.

  a. Write   b. No write   c. Writes

14. Close the windows and _____ the door.

  a. opened   b. open   c. opens

15. _____ aware of everything around you.

  a. Be   b. No be   c. Is

Ability and Possibility

Making Connections

Can and *Could* for Ability and Possibility

1 Complete the sentences with *can*, *could*, *can't*, or *couldn't* and the verbs in parentheses.

Technology and Fun

WebFriends.cambridge.org asked its customers to write about how they use technology for social purposes. Here is what they wrote:

Janet: On this site, I __can meet__ (meet) other people online who like to watch
(1)
movies. Five years ago, I _____ (not do) this because my Internet
(2)
connection was slow. Today, I _____ (discuss) movies with people
(3)
all over the world. We _____ (share) movies with each other, and I
(4)
_____ (make) my movie collection bigger.
(5)

Robert: I'm 13 years old. Two years ago, I _____ (not use) the
(6)
Internet. My parents said I was too young. They said I _____ (read)
(7)
books or watch TV instead. Today, I _____ (not download) movies
(8)
and share music because my parents don't let me. I _____ (chat) with
(9)
my friends online, but I _____ (not talk) with them after 8:00 p.m.
(10)
Those are the rules in my house.

---

2 Read the chart about Maria, Jim, and Ana's abilities with technology in the past and in the present. Write sentences with *can* (*not*) and *could* (*not*). Use the information from the table.

	Maria		Jim and Ana	
	Today	Last Year	Today	Last Year
Upload photos	Yes	Yes	Yes	No
Send text messages	No	No	Yes	Yes
Meet friends online	Yes	No	Yes	Yes
Share music online	Yes	Yes	No	No
Create a blog	Yes	No	No	No

1. Today / Maria / upload photos

   Today Maria can upload photos.

2. Last year / Jim and Ana / upload photos

   Last year Jim and Ana could not upload photos.

3. Today / Maria / send text messages

   _____

4. Last year / Jim and Ana / send text messages

   _____

5. Last year / Maria / meet friends online

   _____

6. Today / Jim and Ana / meet friends online

   _____

7. Today / Jim and Ana / share music online

   _____

8. Last year / Maria / share music online

   _____

9. Last year / Jim and Ana / create a blog

   _____

10. Today / Maria / create a blog

   _____

3 Write questions using *can* and *could* from the answers below. Use the words in bold to help you.

1. **Q:** (Where / you) *Where can you find a website to share music?*

   A: You can **find a website to share music** at www.Musicshare.cambridge.org.

2. **Q:** (you) _____

   A: **No**, you could not **buy music on the Internet 25 years ago**.

3. **Q:** (Where / I) _____

   A: You can **share vacation pictures** on free photo sites.

4. **Q:** (I) _____

   A: **Yes**, you can **take videos with some cell phones**.

5. **Q:** (you) _____

   A: **Yes**, I could **send text messages on my old cell phone**.

6. **Q:** (How / people) _____

   A: People can **organize their e-mail** with different folders.

7. **Q:** (When / I) _____

   A: You can **buy the new spy movie on DVD** next weekend.

8. **Q:** (you) _____

   A: **Yes**, I can **recommend a good business networking site**.

4 Write true sentences about how you and people you know use technology. Use *can*, *can't*, *could*, or *couldn't*.

1. Today, I *can text message* .

2. A few years ago, my friends *couldn't chat online* .

3. Now, I _____ .

4. Last year, I _____ .

5. Today my best friend _____ .

6. About 10 years ago, my best friend _____ .

Be Able To and Know How To for Ability

1 Change *can* to *be able to* and *can't* to *not be able to*. Use the verbs in bold.

1. José can **purchase** a book online.

   José _is able to purchase_ a book online.

2. Lara and Rina can't **apply** for a bank account online.

   Lara and Rina _____ for a bank account online.

3. Paola can **take** pictures with her cell phone.

   Paola _____ pictures with her cell phone.

4. She can't **make** a video call with her cell phone.

   She _____ a video call with her cell phone.

5. Jim and Julie can **read** the news online

   Jim and Julie _____ the news online.

6. They can't **record** music online.

   They _____ music online.

7. Mahmud can **look** at pictures on his computer.

   Mahmud _____ at pictures on his computer.

8. He can't **watch** TV on his computer.

   He _____ TV on his computer.

2 Complete the sentences with the correct form of *be able to* or *know how to* and the verbs in parentheses.

1. Ricky _does not know how to design_ (not know how to / design) a website.

2. Susan _____ (be able to / make) phone calls on the Internet.

3. I _____ (not be able to / call) my family on my laptop.

4. The students in my class _____ (know how to / post) comments on our class blog.

5. My brothers _____ (know how to / download) music from the Internet.

6. We _____ (not know how to / check) that the information on a website is accurate.

7. My uncle _____ (not be able to / attach) a file to his e-mail.

8. Pablo _____ (know how to / use) e-readers.

3 How good are you with technology? Write the questions for the technology questionnaire. Use *know how to* and *be able to* with *you* and the information from the box below. Check *Yes* or *No*.

Be able to	Know how to
1. Shop online	5. Order food online
2. Check your grades online	6. Take pictures with a cell phone
3. Record videos with your cell phone	7. Use video chats with your classmates
4. Pay your bills online	8. Sell used books online

Questionnaire

		Yes	No
1.	*Are you able to shop online?*	❑	❑
2.		❑	❑
3.		❑	❑
4.		❑	❑
5.		❑	❑
6.		❑	❑
7.		❑	❑
8.		❑	❑

4 Write sentences that are true for you and the people you know with *be able to* or *know how to*. Use the ideas from the box or your own ideas.

attach a file to an e-mail	send a text message
chat online	upload an assignment to a class website
post a comment on a blog	use an e-reader
search for research topics	write a blog entry

1. I / be able to   *I am able to attach a file to an e-mail.*

2. I / not be able to

3. My friends / know how to

4. My _____ / not know how to   _____

5. I / know how to   _____

6. I / not know how to   _____

7. My friends / be able to   _____

8. My _____ / not be able to   _____

Avoid Common Mistakes

1 Circle the mistakes.

1. Last year, Dan **can send** emails. Now, he **can chat** online, and he **can post** comments
   (a)   (b)   (c)
   on blogs.

2. Jerry **can save** money because he **can make** calls online and **can talks** for a long time.
   (a)   (b)   (c)

3. Ten years ago, they **could keep** in touch easily. They **can write** letters, and they
   (a)   (b)
   could make calls.
   (c)

4. At the library, you **can use** a computer, you **can prepare** a report, and you **can to print**
   (a)   (b)   (c)
   your work.

5. With technology, Lisa **can do** research, she **can share** information, and she
   (a)   (b)
   cans communicate easily.
   (c)

6. Yesterday, I **could uploaded** photos, but I **could not share** them. Today, I
   (a)   (b)
   can share them.
   (c)

7. Asha **can receive** e-mails, and she **cans send** texts with her phone. She
   (a)   (b)
   cannot send photos.
   (c)

8. Businesses **can to communicate** quickly with customers. They **can send** texts, or
   (a)   (b)
   they **can call**.
   (c)

2 Find and correct nine more mistakes in this e-mail from Karen to her professor.

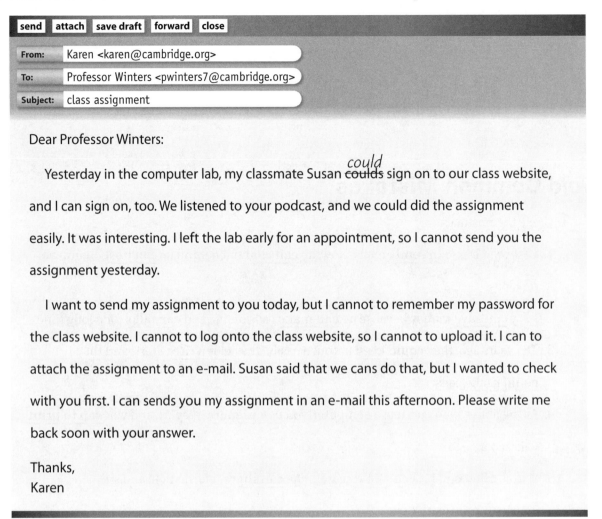

send | attach | save draft | forward | close

From: Karen <karen@cambridge.org>

To: Professor Winters <pwinters7@cambridge.org>

Subject: class assignment

Dear Professor Winters:

    Yesterday in the computer lab, my classmate Susan ~~coulds~~ *could* sign on to our class website, and I can sign on, too. We listened to your podcast, and we could did the assignment easily. It was interesting. I left the lab early for an appointment, so I cannot send you the assignment yesterday.

    I want to send my assignment to you today, but I cannot to remember my password for the class website. I cannot to log onto the class website, so I cannot to upload it. I can to attach the assignment to an e-mail. Susan said that we cans do that, but I wanted to check with you first. I can sends you my assignment in an e-mail this afternoon. Please write me back soon with your answer.

Thanks,
Karen

Self-Assessment

Circle the word or phrase that correctly completes each sentence.

1. James _____ connect with friends through social networking sites.

   a. can to   b. cans   c. can

2. What _____ me about business communication styles today?

   a. you can tell   b. can you tell   c. can you telling

3. Feride's parents _____ an e-mail.

   a. don't know how send   b. don't know how to send   c. didn't know how to sent

4. Maria and Lupe _____ register for classes online.

   a. is able to   b. are able to   c. able to

5. **A:** Can Jane use your laptop? **B:** _____ .

   a. No, she can   b. No, she couldn't   c. No, she can't

6. _____ comments on a blog?

   a. Do you know how make   b. Do you know how   c. Do you know how to make

7. Ten years ago, _____ find an Internet café in your town?

   a. can you   b. could you   c. you could

8. We _____ chat online in the language lab about different topics.

   a. able to   b. are able   c. are able to

9. Oscar _____ share music with his friends.

   a. can't to   b. can   c. couldn't to

10. _____ operate video conferencing software?

    a. Do Ahmed know how to   b. Does Ahmed know to   c. Does Ahmed know how to

11. How _____ using technology?

    a. can you communicate   b. you can communicate   c. can you communicated

12. Janet _____ access the network from her apartment.

    a. isn't able to   b. isn't able   c. isn't can able to

13. _____ provide online advising?

    a. Are your school able   b. Is your school able to   c. Is your school can

14. Last week, Mark _____ the language lab.

    a. could not visit   b. cannot visit   c. could not visited

15. _____ surf the Internet?

    a. Does Ann know how to   b. Does Ann know how   c. Ann know how to

Requests and Permission

College Life

Can, *Could*, and *Would* for Requests

1 Read the two conversations. Complete the sentences with *can, can't, could,* or *would*. Sometimes there is more than one correct answer.

Conversation 1

Mary: Hi, <u>*can* OR *could* OR *would*</u> you help me start my
(1)
research for my economics paper?

Librarian: Of course, what's the topic?

Mary: The history of paper money.

Librarian: OK, first try our online database on economics.

Mary: _____ you show me how to find it?
(2)

Librarian: Certainly. Here on the computer screen, just click on

"databases" and type in your topic.

Mary: _____ you give me access to use this database? I'd like to do some
(3)
research from home.

Librarian: I'm sorry. I _____ . However, the library is open until 2:00 a.m. You can
(4)
come in anytime before then and use it.

Conversation 2

John: Hello. _____ you tell me how to apply for
(5)
financial aid at the college?

Financial Aid Officer: Sure. Just complete the application online.

_____ you give me your e-mail address?
(6)
I can send you the link.

John: Sorry. I'm not very good with computers.

_____ you give me the paper application?
(7)

Financial Aid Officer: No problem. Here it is.

John: Thanks. This is my first time in the financial aid office. _____ you help
_(8)_

me complete the application?

Financial Aid Officer: Of course, just come with me, and I can help you.

2 Write requests with *can*, *could*, and *would*. Use *please* to make polite requests. Sometimes
there is more than one correct answer.

1. Ask someone in the registration office: **Give me information on the English 101 class.**

    Could you give me information on the English 101 class, please?

2. You want to talk to your professor after class. Ask her: **Meet with me after class.**

    _____

3. You enter the computer lab. Ask the technician: **Show me a computer with recording software.**

    _____

4. You are in a study group. Ask a study group member: **Host a study session.**

    _____

5. Ask a manager at the school cafeteria: **Give me the weekend schedule for the cafeteria.**

    _____

6. You enter the tutoring center. Ask a tutor: **Help me with my grammar homework.**

    _____

7. You need a letter from the financial aid office. Ask a counselor: **Write a letter to my bank.**

    _____

8. Your English class has a party on the last day of class. Ask your classmate: **Bring a dish to the party.**

    _____

3 Unscramble the words below to write requests. Sometimes there is more than one
correct answer.

1. come / can / to my office later / you / please   *Can you please come to my office later?*

2. your books / would / close / you   _____

3. you / remove your hat / could / please   _____

4. you / show me the library / can   _____

5. with the printer / please / you / help me / could   _____

6. open your books / you / to page 93 / would   _____

Can, Could, and May for Permission

1 Complete the requests for permission with different people. Use *I* with the words in parentheses. Sometimes there is more than one correct answer.

1. I need more time to finish my paper.

   May I give (give / may) you my paper
   next week?

2. Susan, my car isn't working, and I have to go to

   work. _____ (use / can) your
   car tonight?

3. Ms. Smith, the printer in the lab is broken.

   _____ (print / could) my paper in
   your office?

4. Dr. Clark, I have a family celebration this weekend.

   _____ (miss / may) your class on Friday?

5. Good afternoon. I would like to pay the bill for my classes. _____ (pay / could)
   by credit card?

6. Joe, I hear you have an open room in your apartment. _____ (be / can)
   your roommate?

2 Write the requests for permission for each answer. Use *can*, *could*, and *may*. Use the answers to help you. Sometimes there is more than one correct answer.

1. **Q:** _Can I borrow your dictionary?_   OR _Could I borrow your dictionary?_

   A: Sure, you can borrow my dictionary.

2. **Q:** _____

   A: Of course, you may use the computer.

3. **Q:** _____

   A: Certainly, you can open the window in the classroom.

4. **Q:** _____

   A: Yes, you may take my Spanish 201 class.

5. **Q:** _____

   A: I'm sorry, you may not register online.

6. **Q:** _____

   A: No, you cannot park here. This parking lot is for teachers only.

3 Ask the people below for permission to do something using *can, could,* or *may.* Use the ideas in the box or your own ideas.

borrow your car	leave early today	use the library printer
join your study group	~~talk with you after class~~	visit you tonight

1. To a professor: *Could I talk with you after class?*

2. To a friend: _____

3. To a family member: _____

4. To a boss: _____

5. To a librarian: _____

6. To a classmate: _____

Avoid Common Mistakes

1 Circle the mistakes.

1. **Could you recommend** a math class? **You can help** me register? **Could you give** me

(a)   (b)   (c)
   the schedule?

2. **Would you to explain** that again? **Could you return** my homework? **Could you write** that for me?

(a)   (b)   (c)

3. **Could you help** me? **May you give** the professor my paper? **Can you lend** me today's notes?

(a)   (b)   (c)

4. **Do you show** me the books? **Would you loan** this book to me? **Could you give** me a library card?

(a)   (b)   (c)

5. **Can you lend** me a pen? **Can you study** with me tonight? **Can you to take** notes for me?

(a)   (b)   (c)

6. **Do I can leave** early today? **May I work** from home tomorrow? **Could I take** my vacation soon?

(a)   (b)   (c)

7. **Could you check** my application? **May I send** it to you? **May you show** me the scholarship

(a)   (b)   (c)
   website?

8. **You can drive** me to school? **Could I borrow** five dollars for lunch? **Can you pick** me up

(a)   (b)   (c)
   after class?

2 Correct eight more mistakes in the Spanish professor's e-mail to the study abroad office staff.

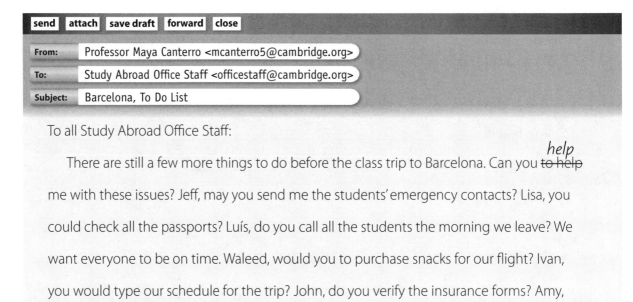

send attach save draft forward close

From: Professor Maya Canterro <mcanterro5@cambridge.org>

To: Study Abroad Office Staff <officestaff@cambridge.org>

Subject: Barcelona, To Do List

To all Study Abroad Office Staff:

There are still a few more things to do before the class trip to Barcelona. Can you ~~to help~~ *help* me with these issues? Jeff, may you send me the students' emergency contacts? Lisa, you could check all the passports? Luís, do you call all the students the morning we leave? We want everyone to be on time. Waleed, would you to purchase snacks for our flight? Ivan, you would type our schedule for the trip? John, do you verify the insurance forms? Amy, can you to remind the students that they can bring only one carry-on bag on the plane? José, you can ask everyone to bring 100 euros? Thank you all for your help!

Professor Maya Canterro

Self-Assessment

Circle the word or phrase that correctly completes each sentence.

1. _____ call you after class?

    a. Can I   b. I would   c. Would I

2. _____ come to your office for help?

    a. I may   b. May I   c. Can I to

3. _____ lend me your accounting book?

    a. You could   b. Do you   c. Could you

4. _____ borrow your laptop?

    a. May I   b. I may   c. Would I

5. _____ return the book I gave you?

    a. Do you   b. Can you   c. You can

6. _____ speak to you about my project?

   a. Could I to   b. Could I   c. Would I

7. _____ show me the computer lab?

   a. Do you   b. You would   c. Would you

8. **A:** Could I see your paper? **B:** _____ .

   a. Sure, you can see it   b. Sure, you do see it   c. Yes, you would

9. _____ pay for the class in three parts?

   a. I can   b. I do   c. Can I

10. _____ give me a receipt for my tuition?

    a. May you   b. Do I   c. Would you

11. **A:** Could you please come to the meeting today? **B:** _____ . I'm busy.

    a. I'm sorry, I don't   b. Of course, I can't   c. I'm sorry, I can't

12. _____ you leave my book on the desk when you are finished?

    a. Do   b. May   c. Could

13. _____ you my work by e-mail?

    a. May I send   b. May send I   c. Could I to send

14. _____ make one more copy of the article for me?

    a. May you   b. You can   c. Can you

15. **A:** Can you help me with this math problem? **B:** _____ .

    a. Yes, I can   b. Yes, I do   c. No, I don't

UNIT 23

Present Progressive
Body Language

Present Progressive Statements

1 Complete the sentences about body language. Use the present progressive form of the verbs in parentheses.

A The salesman _is listening_ (listen) to a customer. The customer _____
(1)   (2)
(explain) that the car is expensive for her. She _____ (show) the palms of
(3)
her hands when she talks. That means she _____ (not lie). The salesman
(4)
_____ (look) down. He seems disappointed.
(5)

B The children _____ (relax) on the floor. The boy _____
(6)   (7)
(not sit) straight. He _____ (rest) his back against the sofa. The girls
(8)
_____ (smile). They _____ (not look) at the boy. The boy
(9)   (10)
_____ (get) bored, but the girls _____ (have) fun.
(11)   (12)

2 Frieda is on the bus. She's leaving a voice mail for her friend on the phone. Complete the sentences with the present progressive form of the verbs in the box.

not pay	send	stare	watch
~~ride~~	sit	text	

Hi Jennifer. I _'m riding_ the bus, and I _____ the people around me. The
(1)   (2)
boy across from me _____ text messages. He _____ at the screen
(3)   (4)
on his phone. He _____ attention to anyone. He _____
(5)   (6)
with his arms close to his body. I think he really likes the person who he _____.
(7)

154

cry	look	move	pick	stand	talk

The women across from me _____ toward the end of the seat. They
                                    (8)

_____ up their backpacks. They _____ at the door. I think that
        (9)   (10)

they're ready to get off the bus. The girl in front _____ near the bus driver.
                                                              (11)

She _____ to him. Her eyes are red. She _____ . I think she's upset.
           (12)   (13)

I wonder why. It's interesting to observe people and how they communicate. Their body

language says a lot.

3 Correct the sentences about each picture below. Write the negative form of the present
progressive, then write affirmative sentences to describe what is really happening. Use the
words given to help you.

Picture A:

1. The woman is buying a car.

   not buy   put / money in the bank

   The woman isn't buying a car.   *She is putting money in the bank.*

2. The man is standing straight.

   not stand   lean / on the counter

   _____   _____

3. The man is talking to the woman.

   not talk   listen / to the woman

   _____   _____

4. The man is crying.

   not cry   smile / at the woman

   _____   _____

Picture B:

5. The mother is hugging her daughter.

not hug

_____

scold[1] / her daughter

_____

6. The girl is nodding her head.

not nod

_____

hold / her head in her hands

_____

7. The mother is laughing.

not laugh

_____

tell / her daughter that she is upset

_____

_____

[1]**scold:** criticize angrily someone who did something wrong

Present Progressive Questions

1 Complete the _Yes / No_ questions about body language with the present progressive form of the verb in parentheses. Then write short answers based on the picture.

1. Q: ___Is___ Tom _leaning_ (lean) against a tree?   A: _Yes, he is._

2. Q: _____ Tom _____ (cross) his legs?   A: _____

3. Q: _____ Tom _____ (talk) on his cell phone?   A: _____

4. Q: _____ Ashley and Lin _____ (sit) at a picnic table?   A: _____

5. Q: _____ Ashley and Lin _____ (look) at each other?   A: _____

6. Q: _____ Ashley and Lin _____ (cry)?   A: _____

7. Q: _____ Ashley _____ (pet) a dog?   A: _____

8. Q: _____ Carla _____ (run) behind Martin?   A: _____

9. Q: _____ Carla _____ (listen) to music?   A: _____

10. Q: _____ Martin _____ (sweat)?   A: _____

2 Read the conversation between two students in class. Write *Yes / No* or information questions with the present progressive. Use the words in parentheses.

Rina: OK, the teacher gave us these three pictures to discuss. Let's look at the body

language in each one.

Max: _Why is the boy resting_ (why / the boy / rest) his head in his hand?
      (1)

Rina: Maybe he's bored.

Max: _____ (he / look) at the clock?
      (2)

Rina: Yes, he is.

Max: _____ (he / think) about leaving the classroom?
      (3)

Rina: Yes, I think so. He probably wants to go home. That is probably what he is

communicating. Look at the next one. _____
                                    (4)

(where / the woman / wait) in line?

Max: At the post office.

Rina: _____ (what / she / do)?
      (5)

Max: She is tapping her foot.

Rina: _____ (why / she / tap) her foot?
      (6)

Max: Maybe she's in a hurry. OK. Here is the last picture.

_____ (where / the people / stand)?
      (7)

Rina: In an office.

Max: _____ (why / the man / move back)?
(8)

Rina: Probably because the woman is standing too close to him.

Max: _____ (they / talk)?
(9)

Rina: Yes, I think so.

Max: _____ (he / make) eye contact with her?
(10)

Rina: No, he's looking down. Maybe he's embarrassed.

3 Write information questions about Paul and Sergio. Use the answers to help you choose the correct *Wh-* words.

1. **A:** (Paul and Sergio / go) _Where are Paul and Sergio going?_ _____
   B: To their class.

2. **A:** (they / study) _____
   B: Psychology.

3. **A:** (they / sit) _____
   B: In the back of the classroom.

4. **A:** (Paul / look at) _____
   B: The teacher.

5. **A:** (Sergio / feel nervous) _____
   B: Because he has an important exam after this class.

6. **A:** (Sergio / bite) _____
   B: His fingernails.

7. **A:** (Paul and Sergio / do) _____
   B: They're tapping their feet.

8. **A:** (Paul / write notes) _____
   B: Because the topic is interesting.

9. **A:** (Paul and Sergio / close their books) _____
   B: Because class is ending.

10. **A:** (Sergio / put his books) _____
    B: In his bag.

Present Progressive and Simple Present

1 Complete the psychology professor's lecture with the present progressive or simple present form of the verbs in parentheses.

_Do_ you usually _look_ (look) at people when you talk? Why _____ people
(1)   (1)   (2)

sometimes _____ (move) their feet? _____ you _____ (touch)
(2)   (3)   (3)

your face right now? Experts agree that body language is a crucial part of communication.

It shows what people _____ (feel) at the moment. People usually _____
                              (4)   (5)

(nod) when they listen. They often _____ (cross) their arms when they don't
                                            (6)

agree. For example, look at Sarah right now. She _____ (lean) forward. That
                                                          (7)

normally _____ (show) that she is interested and feels positive about this subject.
              (8)

Oh, and look at Martin. He _____ (look) out the window. Maybe he's bored.
                                    (9)

And Sylvia _____ (tap) her fingers. Sometimes that _____ (mean) a
                  (10)   (11)

person is nervous. What _____ Tatiana _____ (do) right now? She
                                (12)   (12)

_____ (chew) on her pen. What _____ you _____ (think) that
      (13)   (14)   (14)

means? You can learn a lot when you watch other people's body language.

2 Describe what the people on the train are doing right now and what they do normally.
Use the simple present or present progressive and the words given.

NORMALLY

NOW

1. The woman / stare / at her daughter / right now

   The woman is staring at her daughter right now.

2. The woman and her daughter / frequently / sit / near the window

   _____

3. The boy / sleep / on the train / at the moment

   _____

4. The boy / often / play / a game on the train

_____

5. The businessman / tie / his shoe / right now

_____

6. The businessman / usually / read / the newspaper

_____

7. The father and son / smile / right now

_____

8. The father and son / normally / listen / to music

_____

9. The conductor / talk / with passengers / at the moment

_____

10. The conductor / usually / collect / tickets / without talking

_____

3 A police trainer and a new police officer are watching a video of a police interview with a suspect. Complete their conversation with the present progressive or simple present and the words in parentheses.

Trainer: OK. Let's talk about the suspect's body language in the video.

 What do you see (what / you / see)?
 (1)

Luís: Well, right now _____ (the suspect / hold) his
 (2)

hands under the table. _____ (why / he / do)
 (3)

that?

Trainer: Well, _____ (people / sometimes / put) their
 (4)

hands under the table when they lie.

Luís: OK. Now _____ (he / cross) his arms.
 (5)

_____ (you / think) he feels defensive?
 (6)

Trainer: Maybe. Or maybe _____ (he / not agree) with
 (7)

the officer.

Luís: Now _____ (the suspect / talk) and
(8)

_____ (the officer / nod) his head.
(9)

_____ (why / he / do) that?
(10)

Trainer: Well, right now, _____ (the officer / show) that
(11)

he is a good listener. _____ (he / want) the
(12)

suspect to trust him.

Luís: This is very interesting. I didn't know that body language was so important

in our jobs!

Avoid Common Mistakes

1 Circle the mistakes.

1. Leila **is sitting** next to her friend. They (talking) and they **are watching** TV.
   (a)   (b)   (c)

2. The professor **is teaching** about body language. Some students **are listenning**, and
   (a)   (b)

   others **are sleeping**.
   (c)

3. The girl **playing** with her friend. They **are telling** secrets, and they **are smiling**.
   (a)   (b)   (c)

4. The suspect **is tapping** his foot, and he **is crossing** his arms. The police officer **watch** him.
   (a)   (b)   (c)

5. The teacher **is talking** in class. The students **are takeing** notes. One student
   (a)   (b)

   is not paying attention.
   (c)

6. The boys **are jumping**. They **are listenning** to each other tell jokes and they **are laughing**.
   (a)   (b)   (c)

7. The mother **is making** eye contact with her son. The son **is looking** down, and he **is cry**.
   (a)   (b)   (c)

8. The police officer **talks** with the suspect. The suspect **is holding** his head, and he **is thinking**.
   (a)   (b)   (c)

2 Correct six more mistakes in the interview below.

Interviewer: Dr. Reynolds, I contacted you because you are ~~finish~~ *finishing* a new book on body

language and gestures across cultures. You spoke with a lot of experts

for your book. Can you describe some of the things people do across

cultures?

Dr. Reynolds: Yes. Look at this picture. These men are siting with their legs crossed.

They are talk to each other and they're not smiling. In this next picture,

the boy lifts his grandmother's hand. He is touching it to his head. That

is a sign of respect for older adults in the Philippines. And in the picture

here, a Korean man is offerring his business card to a colleague. He is

useing both hands. This is a sign of respect in business situations. That is

also common in China and Japan.

People from other cultures might get confused by this next photo. Here,

these people in Bulgaria, nod their heads. In parts of Greece, Turkey, and

Bulgaria people nod to say "no."

Interviewer: Wow! Body language really is different around the world.

Self-Assessment

Circle the word or phrase that correctly completes each sentence.

1. _____ right now?

   a. What are you doing   b. What do you do   c. What you doing

2. Kim _____ her backpack slowly.

   a. is open   b. is opening   c. is openning

3. Mark often _____ his boss on the bus and gets nervous.

   a. is seeing   b. is see   c. sees

4. _____ your arms when you are angry?

   a. Are you crossing   b. Do you cross   c. You cross

5. Marta _____ her report on body language.

   a. type   b. is typeing   c. is typing

6. The woman _____ money in her hand.

   a. is hold   b. is holding   c. holding

7. _____ to on her cell phone? She looks upset.

   a. Who is Tonya talking   b. Who Tonya talks   c. Who Tonya talking

8. Tom _____ his arms. Is he defensive?

   a. crossing   b. is crossing   c. cross

9. The suspects _____ the truth. They are not making eye contact.

   a. are not tell   b. not telling   c. are not telling

10. _____ the suspect?

    a. What is the policeman ask   b. What is the policeman asking   c. What the policeman asks

11. Gestures often _____ from culture to culture.

    a. are varying   b. vary   c. are vary

12. _____ about body language in her class this semester?

    a. Is she learn   b. Does she learning   c. Is she learning

13. She _____ her head because she understands.

    a. is noding   b. nodding   c. is nodding

14. The boy can't concentrate right now. He _____ out the window.

    a. is look   b. looks   c. is looking

15. _____ her hand on her chin?

    a. Why does she have   b. Why is she having   c. Why she has

Past Progressive and Simple Past

Inventions and Discoveries

Past Progressive

1 Complete the paragraph about the California Gold Rush. Use the past progressive form of the verbs in parentheses.

In January of 1848, James Wilson Marshall and his workers _were building_ (build) (1) a sawmill[1] near Sacramento, California. He _____ (not look) for gold. (2) However, one day he _____ (3) (walk) by the river near the sawmill. By coincidence, he _____ (stare) into the (4) water. He saw some pieces of gold. He picked up the gold and showed it to his workers. Soon his workers _____ (find) gold, too. They didn't keep the gold a secret. They (5) told other people in Sacramento and San Francisco. Soon the news traveled everywhere.

People _____ (arrive) from all over the country and the world to (6) look for gold. By December of 1849, thousands of people _____ (7) (search) for gold. However, not everyone found gold. By 1855, when the gold rush ended, people found about $2 billion in gold.

---

[1]**sawmill:** place where people cut wood into boards or other forms, usually with heavy machinery

2 Write affirmative and negative sentences with the past progressive about life in the 1950s in the United States. Write affirmative sentences when you see ✓. Write negative sentences when you see ✗.

1. Dwight Eisenhower / lead / the United States (✓)

   Dwight Eisenhower was leading the United States.

2. Gasoline / sell / for $2.00 a gallon (✗)

   _____

3. Teenagers / listen / to hip-hop music (✗)

   _____

4. The post office / charge / three cents for a stamp (✓)

   _____

5. Millions of people / buy / their first TV (✓)

   _____

6. The United States / celebrate / its 200th anniversary (✗)

   _____

7. Americans / drink / the first diet soda (✓)

   _____

8. Students / surf / the Internet (✗)

   _____

9. The average teacher / earn / $15,000 a year (✗)

   _____

10. Banks / offer / credit cards for use at different companies / for the first time (✓)

   _____

3 Answer the questions with information that is true for you. Use the past progressive.

1. **Q:** What were you doing at 6:00 a.m. this morning?

   A: _I was sleeping._

2. **Q:** What was your best friend doing last night?

   A: _____

3. **Q:** What were you doing on Sunday evening?

   A: _____

4. **Q:** What were your classmates doing in class this week?

   A: _____

5. **Q:** What was the teacher doing at the beginning of your last class?

   A: _____

Time Clauses with Past Progressive and Simple Past

1 Complete the sentences. Use the past progressive or the simple past.

In 1893, Milton Hershey_ *visited* _(visit) the Chicago World Fair. While he _____
(1)   (2)
(look) at the many exhibits, he _____ (see) a German chocolate maker. He
(3)

_____ (become) interested in the chocolate and _____ (want) to
(4)   (5)
make it. He knew that the demand for chocolate _____ (grow) at the time. He soon
(6)

_____ (start) a chocolate company. While he _____ (experiment) with
(7)   (8)
milk chocolate, he _____ (discover) the perfect formula of milk, sugar, and cocoa.
(9)

Soon the company _____ (produce) a lot of chocolate bars. Before long, people all
(10)

over the country _____ (eat) chocolate bars from the Hershey Chocolate Company.
(11)

2 Complete the paragraph from a story about the invention of Ivory soap. Use the past progressive and simple past in each sentence.

In 1878, a worker at a soap factory _ *was stirring* _(stir) soap with a machine when the lunch
(1)

bell _____ (ring). He went for lunch, but he forgot to turn off the machine. During
(2)

lunch, while the machine _____ (mix) the soap, too much air _____ (enter)
(3)   (4)

the mixture. When the worker returned, he discovered the soap was filled with air. The worker

decided that his error was not a problem. He finished the soap with the error, and the company sold

it. Soon people bought the soap. While they _____ (use) it, they _____ (find)
(5)   (6)

that it could float in water. They liked that and wrote letters to thank the company for this new

floating soap. This worker's error created a very popular kind of soap.

3 Complete the sentences about another invention. Use the simple past and past progressive and the words in parentheses.

In 1975, _Gary and his friends were having_ (Gary and his friends / have) dinner one night
(1)

_____ (when they / start) talking about pets. They talked about
(2)

the problems of owning a pet. Pets were expensive. They needed a lot of care.

_____ (while / his friends / discuss) their pets,
(3)

_____ (Gary / think) of the perfect pet. The perfect pet didn't need food. It didn't
(4)

need attention. It didn't need anything. _____ (when / a friend
(5)

ask) him about his perfect pet, _____ (Gary / tell) him that his pet was a rock.
(6)

_____ (when / Gary / describe) the many advantages of a pet
(7)

rock, _____ (his friends / laugh). They didn't think he was
(8)

serious.

A few months later, the pet rocks were in the stores. The rocks cost less than four dollars. Everyone

wanted one. Gary Dahl became a millionaire in less than six months.

Avoid Common Mistakes

1 Circle the mistakes.

1. What (they were doing)? **He was riding** his bike. **She was playing** with friends.
   (a)   (b)   (c)

2. **Dinh was thinking** about the problem. **He were trying** solutions. **They were not working**.
   (a)   (b)   (c)

3. What **was the teacher saying**? **She was talking** about history, and **she explaining** the test.
   (a)   (b)   (c)

4. **Mr. Hershey was experimenting** with chocolate. **He was making** it into a bar.
   (a)   (b)

   People was buying it.
   (c)

5. **A:** What **you were doing** at 8:00 p.m.? **B: I was reading**, and **the radio was playing** my favorite song.
   (a)   (b)   (c)

6. **A:** Where **you were going**? **B: I was going** to the store, and **Matt was walking** to the library.
   (a)   (b)   (c)

7. **We were visiting** the museum. **We was looking** at an invention, and **we were reading** about
   (a)   (b)   (c)

   its history.

8. **I was studying** with friends. **We were discussing** inventors. **We were learn** about inventions.
   (a)   (b)   (c)

2 Correct seven more mistakes in the conversation about the history of the popsicle.

                       was looking

Hiro: Hey, Bruna, I ~~looking~~ for a book, and I saw you in the library yesterday.

           What you were doing?

Bruna: I was write about the history of the popsicle. It's amazing. One day, a boy playing. He was

           thirsty and made a fruit drink. He accidentally left the drink outside with a small stick in it

           to stir it. That night, while he were sleeping, the temperature dropped below freezing. The

           next morning, he went outside and saw his drink was frozen. He tasted it, and it was great!

           Eighteen years later, he was looking for a new business idea. He remembered the frozen

           fruit drink and started a popsicle business. Soon the company was produce seven flavors.

           People was buying them, and they was telling others about them. By 1928, the company

           sold over 60 million popsicles.

Self-Assessment

Circle the word or phrase that correctly completes each sentence.

1. Mark _____ with chocolate.

   a. experimenting   b. was experimenting   c. was experiment

2. **A:** Were they looking for gold? **B:** _____ .

   a. Yes, they was   b. No, they wasn't   c. Yes, they were

3. While he _____ his textbook, he understood the problem.

   a. was reading   b. was read   c. reading

4. When Mara entered the office, she _____ the new secretary.

   a. was seeing   b. sees   c. saw

5. When Lana _____ the discovery, she was working at home.

   a. make   b. was making   c. made

6. _____ new discoveries during the 2000s?

   a. Was Dr. Carpenter   b. Dr. Carpenter   c. Was Dr. Carpenter
       research   researching   researching

7. Dr. Carpenter _____ for a solution.

   a. wasn't look   b. were not looking   c. was not looking

8. He thought about the problem _____ .

   a. when was he reading   b. when he was read   c. when he was reading

9. _____ to find?

   a. What was the   b. What the   c. What the researcher
      researcher trying   researcher trying   was trying

10. Bob was making coffee _____ he got a new idea for an invention.

    a. while   b. how   c. when

11. **A:** Were you listening to the news report? **B:** _____ .

    a. Yes, we weren't   b. No, we aren't   c. Yes, we were

12. _____ sticky papers for bookmarks.

    a. John weren't using   b. John not using   c. John was not using

13. Jorge was doing research in the lab when he _____ a new medicine.

    a. discovered   b. was discovering   c. discovers

14. Ruth Wakefield _____ chocolate chip cookies at her restaurant.

    a. were bake   b. was baking   c. were baking

15. While _____ in the library, I met a friend.

    a. I was studying   b. I studying   c. was I studying

Subject and Object Pronouns

1 Complete the chart with the missing pronouns.

Subject Pronouns	Object Pronouns
I	1. *me*
2.	you
3.	him
she	4.
it	5.
we	6.
they	7.

2 Complete the sentences with subject and object pronouns. Look at the bold words to help you.

1. I eat **fast food**. Do you eat _*it*_ ?

2. I eat **vegetables**. _____ are good for your health.

3. **Maria** enjoys soda. _____ also drinks coffee.

4. **Fast-food restaurants** are very popular. Do you eat at _____ ?

5. **Marcos** loves both chicken and fish. Should _____ eat them five times a week?

6. My friends ate **clams** last night. They didn't like _____ .

7. I sent **you** some healthy recipes. Did _____ use them?

8. **Linda** cooked all the meals this week. Did you tell _____ that you liked them?

9. Hi, James. **Sandra and I** were in the supermarket last night. Did you see _____ ?

10. Here is a list of the ingredients that **Richard** needs. Could you buy them for _____ ?

11. **Paul and I** were in the cafeteria yesterday. _____ had lunch with your sister.

12. **I** am making dinner now. Can you help _____ ?

3 Read the paragraphs and circle the correct subject and object pronouns.

The Slow Food Movement

Slow food is not only the opposite of fast food.

Slow Food is also an international organization.

Carlo Petrini started **(it)/ him** in 1986. **Him / He**
(1)   (2)

taught people that fast food and a fast life can hurt

they / them. **Him / He** wanted people to cook and
(3)   (4)

enjoy the experience of food. Many people agreed

with **he / him**.
(5)

Today Petrini's organization has over 100,000 members. **Them / They** live in 153 different
(6)

countries. The Slow Food movement teaches people about food. **It / He** encourages everyone
(7)

to eat fresh and local foods. These foods can help you in many ways. **Them / They** keep
(8)

him / you healthy. **It / They** fight sickness. They give **we / us** important nutrients.
(9)   (10)   (11)

My friend Ann found out about the Slow Food movement this year. **She / Her** started a
(12)

local community organization about the movement. Ann told **me / I** about Slow Food, and
(13)

now **I / me** am a part of the community organization, too. Now Ann and **I / me** are big fans of
(14)   (15)

Carlo Petrini. Slow Food teaches **we / us** to appreciate our food. **We / Us** can all eat better and
(16)   (17)

enjoy our food more.

4 Read the questions. Write answers that are true for you. Replace the words in bold with the
correct subject and object pronouns.

1. **Q:** Do **you** see **your doctor** regularly?   **A:** _Yes, I see her regularly._

2. **Q:** Do **you** eat **fresh vegetables** often?   **A:** _____

3. **Q:** Do **your friends** eat with **you**?   **A:** _____

4. **Q:** Do **you** drink **coffee**?   **A:** _____

5. **Q:** Is **soda** good for **you and your friends**?   **A:** _____

Questions About the Subject and the Object

1 Write information questions about subjects and objects. Use the bold words in each answer to help you write the questions. Some questions are in the simple present, and some are in the simple past.

1. **Q:** *What tastes delicious?*   **A: The hamburgers** taste delicious.

2. **Q:** _____ **A:** Becky baked **bread**.

3. **Q:** _____ **A: Hinda** ate with Jane.

4. **Q:** _____ **A:** She met **Mark** at the store.

5. **Q:** _____ **A: My mother** serves healthy food.

6. **Q:** _____ **A:** Beans provide **important nutrients**.

7. **Q:** _____ **A: Americans** eat a lot of meat.

8. **Q:** _____ **A:** My father drinks **green tea**.

9. **Q:** _____ **A: Jim** looks healthy.

10. **Q:** _____ **A:** Alem ordered **fish**.

11. **Q:** _____ **A: Tom** read a blog on baking.

12. **Q:** _____ **A: Fast food** has many calories.

2 Unscramble the words to form questions about subjects and objects.

1. did / what / Ali / for breakfast / have   *What did Ali have for breakfast?*

2. a healthy breakfast / ate / who _____

3. do / promote / some chefs / what _____

4. promotes / who / healthy food / for children _____

5. contain / fresh food / does / what _____

6. do / what / contain / smoothies _____

7. eats / who / vegetarian food at school _____

8. Jin / cook for dinner / does / what _____

9. is / what / your favorite dish _____

10. did / at the restaurant / who / see / you _____

3 Write questions about the food in the picture. Use the information given. Then write the short answer to each question. Use the simple past.

	Question	Short Answer
1. **Q:** (who / make / a salad)	_Who made a salad?_	**A:** _Carla did._
2. **Q:** (what / Carla / make)	_____	**A:** _____
3. **Q:** (who / bring / cake)	_____	**A:** _____
4. **Q:** (what / Brian / bring)	_____	**A:** _____
5. **Q:** (who / cook / pasta)	_____	**A:** _____
6. **Q:** (what / Hannah / cook)	_____	**A:** _____
7. **Q:** (who / prepare / fried chicken)	_____	**A:** _____
8. **Q:** (what / Nick / prepare)	_____	**A:** _____

4 Write questions about food. Then ask a friend. Write his or her answers.

1. **Q:** _____What did you_____ (you) eat for lunch today?   **A:** _I ate fish._

2. **Q:** _____Who_____ in your family likes chocolate?   **A:** _My sister does._

3. **Q:** _____ (you) have for breakfast yesterday?   **A:** _____

4. **Q:** _____ in your family drinks coffee in the morning?   **A:** _____

5. **Q:** _____ (you) buy at the supermarket last week?   **A:** _____

6. **Q:** _____ (you) eat lunch with during the week?   **A:** _____

Avoid Common Mistakes

1 Circle the mistakes.

1. **My sister and I** drink smoothies. (He) likes banana smoothies, and **I** like strawberry smoothies.
   (a)   (b)   (c)

2. Processed foods are not healthy for **me**. **They** have many calories, but **me** like them.
   (a)   (b)   (c)

3. Paul buys food that is good for **her**. **He** doesn't eat candy, but **he** likes it.
   (a)   (b)   (c)

4. Many of **us** eat healthy food. **We** are busy, but **us** make time to shop and cook.
   (a)   (b)   (c)

5. I'm worried about my parents. **They** make unhealthy choices. **Them** eat things that are bad for **them**.
   (a)   (b)   (c)

6. **She doesn't use recipes. Laura** cooks without help. **Her** family loves the food she makes for **them**.
   (a)   (b)   (c)

7. My parents and **me** like ice cream. **We** eat **it** every night.
   (a)   (b) (c)

8. I bought the apples for **her. Tanya** likes fruit. **She** enjoys it when **she** wants a snack.
   (a)   (b)   (c)

2 Read the text a student wrote for her English class about ways to eat healthier food. Find and correct the mistakes.

>   We have very busy lives and full schedules these days. ~~Us~~ *We* need easy ways to make good decisions about food.
>
>   My husband and me make a list before us go shopping. Supermarkets want us to buy junk food. They put those items in the front of the store. They make it easy for we to buy them. However, we only buy food that is on our list. Also, my family and I don't buy processed foods. We buy fresh, natural food items. Them are healthy, and they taste good.
>
>   She has another way to make good choices. My friend Irina doesn't buy food at work or school. Her schedule allows her to prepare and bring her own lunches. He has more control of what her eats.
>
>   Try these tips the next time you make a choice about food.

Self-Assessment

Circle the word or phrase that correctly completes each sentence.

1. _____ fast food?

   a. Who enjoys   b. Who does enjoy   c. What did enjoy

2. I made my brother pizza. _____ liked it.

   a. He   b. Him   c. She

3. Schools want students to eat healthy food. They make special menus for _____ .

   a. they   b. it   c. them

4. **A:** Who had the banana? **B:** Carlos _____ .

   a. does   b. did   c. can

5. My brother visited _____ for dinner last night.

   a. my wife and I   b. my wife and me   c. we

6. Terry uses recipes from her mother. She likes _____ because they are easy to follow.

   a. her   b. it   c. them

7. Please choose anything you want from the menu. _____ good to you?

   a. Who did look   b. What looks   c. What does look

8. _____ made a delicious dinner for our roommate.

   a. My brother and I   b. My brother and me   c. I and my brother

9. I enjoy fast-food restaurants. _____ are quick and easy.

   a. They   b. It   c. Them

10. _____ to eat for breakfast?

    a. What you like   b. Who like   c. What do you like

11. We told Mike not to order the fish, but he didn't listen to _____ .

    a. us   b. her   c. we

12. Carol created a delicious new dish. She served _____ to me yesterday.

    a. they   b. it   c. them

13. Who _____ processed food?

    a. does like   b. do you like   c. likes

14. **A:** Who eats salad every day? **B:** _____ .

    a. Ray does   b. Ray do   c. Ray did

15. I got the carrots for John. _____ likes them.

    a. She   b. Him   c. He

Infinitives and Gerunds

Do What You Enjoy Doing

Infinitives

1 Complete the sentences with the infinitive form of the verbs in the boxes.

~~be~~	look	put	swim	teach

Jessi Walter loves _____*to be*_____ around children.
(1)
After she graduated from college, she worked in a big financial

company. Then she lost her job and started _____
(2)
for another job. While she was looking for a job, she

gave swimming lessons to children. The children learned

_____ quickly. Jessi discovered that she liked
(3)
_____ children. Jessi was also a great cook. She
(4)
decided _____ her two interests together.
(5)

combine	make	receive	share	work

Jessi continued _____ with children, but in a new way. She began
(6)
_____ cupcakes with children. Soon, she opened a new business called
(7)
Cupcake Kids (now called Taste Buds). With this new business, Jessi was able

_____ her love for cooking with her love for children, and in her classes she
(8)
showed them that cooking can be fun. She didn't expect _____ so much
(9)
attention for her new business. *New York Magazine* put her business on its "Best of New

York" list. When Jessi started, she hoped _____ her love for children with her
(10)
love for cooking. She succeeded, and now she loves her job.

2 A Complete the sentences with simple present verbs followed by infinitives. Use the words in parentheses.

1. Gustavo _needs to make_ (need / make) money.

2. He _____ (like / play) with dogs.

3. He _____ (want / find) a way to make money with dogs.

4. He _____ (hope / walk) his neighbors' dogs when they are at work.

5. The neighbors _____ (prefer / have) help with their dogs during the day.

6. This is perfect for Gustavo, so he _____ (decide / talk) to the neighbors as soon as possible.

B Complete the sentences with simple past verbs followed by infinitives. Use the words in parentheses.

1. Pam _loved to sing_ (love / sing) as a child.

2. She also _____ (learn / dance) as a child.

3. However, she _____ (hate / play) the piano.

4. When she was in college, Pam

_____ (try / get) a part in a play.

5. She _____ (need / sing) when she tried out for the play.

6. Pam got the part, and she

_____ (begin / practice) every day.

7. The play was a big success, and Pam

_____ (continue / be) in many plays after that.

3 Complete the conversation using the words in parentheses. Use contractions when possible.

Marissa: Hi, Professor Ruiz. _I love to practice_ (I / love / practice) my Spanish. It's one of
          (1)
my hobbies. _____ (I / would like / find) a way to practice
                   (2)
more.

Professor Ruiz: _____ (would like / you / join) the Spanish Club on
                   (3)
our trip to a *tapas* restaurant next Monday night? _____
                                              (4)
(the club / decided / try) a place where we can continue to use our Spanish outside
of class.

Marissa: Yes, _____ (I / would like / go).
               (5)
_____ (I / expect / be) free that night.
          (6)
_____ (I / not want / miss) a chance to speak Spanish.
          (7)

Professor Ruiz: Great! _____ (you / need / send) an e-mail to Roberto, the
               (8)
president of the club. He can help you.

Marissa: That's easy. Also, _____ (I / would prefer / bring) a friend
                   (9)
with me. Is that OK?

Professor Ruiz: I think so. _____ (I / plan / see) Roberto later today.
               (10)
I can ask him.

Marissa: _____ (I / hate / have) you do that for me.
          (11)

Professor Ruiz: It's no problem. _____ (I / hope / talk) with you
               (12)
later today.

4 Complete the sentences with information that is true for you. Use infinitives.

1. I love _to play soccer_ _____.

2. My best friend plans _____.

3. My teacher decided _____.

4. I refuse _____.

5. I learned _____.

Gerunds

1 Complete the sentences with simple past verbs followed by gerunds. Use the words in parentheses.

David and Alan were roommates at a university in Texas. They _liked studying_ (like / study), but they
(1)
_____ (prefer / play) video games.
(2)
They played for many hours each day. As soon as they finished their classes, they _____ (start / play).
(3)
Sometimes they _____ (avoid / do)
(4)
their assignments. They often _____ (not stop / play) until late
(5)
at night. The roommates became very good at the games, and if the games broke, they
learned to fix them. They _____ (enjoy / fix) broken games.
(6)
They _____ (begin / buy) broken video games. Soon, they
(7)
_____ (start / sell) the video games they fixed. They were making
(8)
money, and their small business _____ (keep / grow). Today,
(9)
they have a big business selling video games, and they make over a million dollars a year.

2 Complete the sentences with the gerund or infinitive forms of the words in parentheses.

1. Alma wants _____ to learn _____ (learn) Japanese.

2. When she learns Japanese, she plans _____ (travel) to Japan on business.

3. She imagines _____ (be) an international sales manager someday.

4. Nora enjoyed _____ (paint) as a child.

5. She stopped _____ (paint) in college.

6. Today, Nora is a successful businesswoman, but she wants _____ (paint) again.

7. She'd like _____ (start) painting again. It can help her relax.

8. Diego doesn't enjoy _____ (live) in his city because it rains a lot.

9. He avoids _____ (go) outside when it rains.

10. He doesn't want _____ (get) wet.

11. He tries _____ (stay) inside until the rain stops.

3 Write sentences about three people's likes and dislikes. Use gerunds or infinitives. Sometimes both are correct.

A 1. Akiko / likes / make clothes

_Akiko likes to make clothes._____ OR _Akiko likes making clothes._____

2. She / enjoys / sew

_She enjoys sewing._____

3. She / want / sell / her designs to a big fashion company

_____

B 4. Yolanda / loves / cook

_____

5. Her sister / prefers / bake

_____

6. Yolanda / does not miss / work / long hours in the bakery

_____

7. Someday / Yolanda and her sister / hope / open / a restaurant

_____

C 8. Dao / began / swim / when she was a child

_____

9. She / kept / swim / throughout college

_____

10. She / would like / be / on the Olympic swim team

_____

4 Complete the sentences with information that is true for you. Use gerunds or infinitives.

1. I hate _working in an office_____ .

2. My best friend avoids _____ .

3. I imagine _____ .

4. I enjoy _____ .

5. I continue _____ .

Avoid Common Mistakes

1 Circle the mistakes.

1. I (wanna find) a new hobby. I **enjoy playing** the guitar, and I **like to sing**.
   　　(a)　　　　　　　　　　　　　(b)　　　　　　　　　　　　(c)

2. Lily **learned to take** photos. She **hated to take** photos of people, but she **loved take** photos
   　　　　(a)　　　　　　　　　　　　　(b)　　　　　　　　　　　　　　　　　(c)
   of animals.

3. **I'd like to make** money. **I'd like to enjoy** my job, and **I like to have** a successful business someday.
   　　(a)　　　　　　　　　　　(b)　　　　　　　　　　　　　(c)

4. **A:** Do you **want to go** to the library? **B:** I **prefer going** later, but I think Rob and Bill **wanna go** now.
   　　　　　　　　(a)　　　　　　　　　　　　　(b)　　　　　　　　　　　　　　　　(c)

5. James **likes to play** video games. He always **needs win**. He **hates to lose**.
   　　　　(a)　　　　　　　　　　　　　　　　(b)　　　　　(c)

6. My sisters **plan starting** a new business. They **hope to make** it successful.
   　　　　　(a)　　　　　　　　　　　　　　　(b)
   They **want to make** money.
   　　　(c)

7. Akiko **enjoyed to sew**. She **loved to make** clothes. She **imagined being** a fashion designer.
   　　　　(a)　　　　　　　(b)　　　　　　　　　　　(c)

8. I **want to find** a new job. **I'd like to do** something fun. **I like to become** a ski instructor.
   　(a)　　　　　　　　　(b)　　　　　　　　　　　(c)

2 Read Luz's blog entry about how she turned her hobby into a successful career. Find and correct nine more mistakes.

○ ○ ○

From Hobby to Career

I'd like to
~~I like to~~ tell you a story about following your dreams. I like to start by telling you

about my family. I come from a big family, and my mother always enjoyed to take

pictures of her children. When I got older, my mother showed me how to use the

camera. I learned taking good pictures. My mother kept to take pictures of our family's

daily life. However, I preferred take pictures of landscapes and nature scenes. I enjoyed

to use a camera. It became my hobby. When I studied photography in college, I wanted

to travel around the world and take pictures. When I finished to study, I got a job with a

famous nature magazine. Now, I do just what I hoped doing. I love my job. I wanna do

this forever. So set your goals high, and you can watch your dreams come true, too.

Self-Assessment

Circle the word or phrase that correctly completes each sentence.

1. Today children enjoy _____ social networking sites.

   a. to use   b. to using   c. using

2. Ben and Sean stopped _____ to school and started a business.

   a. going   b. to go   c. go

3. Jessica expects _____ expensive clothes with a big fashion designer someday.

   a. design   b. to design   c. designing

4. I told my friends that next summer I _____ at a national park.

   a. would like volunteer   b. like to volunteer   c. would like to volunteer

5. When Raúl left his country, he missed _____ his family every day.

   a. seeing   b. to see   c. see

6. James and his sister _____ in London next semester.

   a. wanna study   b. want to study   c. want studying

7. When do you hope _____ your new business?

   a. starting   b. to starting   c. to start

8. Jon refused _____ a car because the public transportation system was good.

   a. to buy   b. to buying   c. buy

9. Sonia prefers _____ at the computer lab in the afternoon.

   a. work   b. working   c. to working

10. _____ your own website?

    a. You like to design   b. Would you like designing   c. Would you like to design

11. The students avoid _____ TV when they have to study for a test.

    a. watching   b. to watch   c. watch

12. Erica and Liz want to learn more about computers. They _____ computer programmers.

    a. like to become   b. would like becoming   c. would like to become

13. David _____ how to swim.

    a. didn't wanna learn   b. didn't wanna to learn   c. didn't want to learn

14. Vladimir _____ his computer business.

    a. would like to sell   b. like to sell   c. would like sell

15. Kim keeps _____ many hours so she can save money.

    a. to work   b. working   c. work

Future with *Be Going To*, Present Progressive, and *Will*

Future with *Be Going To* or Present Progressive

1 Complete the sentences with *be going to* or the present progressive. Sometimes both are possible.

Future Plans Already Made

Philippe just got a new job as an editor at a publishing company in New York. He already started the job, and he __*is moving*__ (move) his family
(1)
there very soon. They already have their plane tickets. They _____ (leave)
(2)
on the 15th of next month. Philippe has a lot to do before his family arrives. This week, he _____ (look) for an
(3)
apartment in the city. His real estate[1] agent _____ (show) him some
(4)
apartments. They _____ (visit) two apartments this afternoon. They
(5)
_____ (not look) at any apartments tomorrow.
(6)

Future Plans

In a few days, Philippe and his real estate agent _____ (see) more
(7)
apartments. However, his agent _____ (not show) him too many
(8)
apartments because Philippe is busy with his new job. He _____
(9)
(take) pictures of each apartment. He _____ (e-mail) them to his
(10)
wife. He _____ (call) his family after he sees all the apartments.
(11)
When they make their decision, they _____ (send) their furniture to
(12)
the new place, and Philippe _____ (start) painting the apartment.
(13)
They are very excited about this move.

---
[1]**real estate:** property like land or buildings

2 Complete the sentences with *be going to* or the present progressive.

Jeff: _Are you going to run_ (be going to: you / run)
$\quad\quad$ (1)

in a race next year?

Erkan: Yes, _____ (present
$\quad\quad\quad\quad\quad\quad$ (2)

progressive: I / start) my training next week.

Jeff: How _____ (present
$\quad\quad\quad\quad\quad$ (3)

progressive: you / train)?

Erkan: _____ (be going to: My
$\quad\quad\quad\quad\quad$ (4)

friend and I / run) between 6 and 12 miles each day.

Jeff: _____ (be going to: you / eat) anything special during your training?
$\quad\quad\quad$ (5)

Erkan: No, _____ (be going to: we / not change) our diets, but
$\quad\quad\quad\quad\quad$ (6)

_____ (be going to: we / increase) the amount of calories we
$\quad\quad$ (7)

eat every day.

3 Write sentences with the present progressive for future plans already made using the words in column 1. Then write sentences with *be going to* for future plans using the words in column 2.

	Future Plans Already Made	Future Plans
1. Linda	visit her family tonight	not travel to Paris next week
2. Aaron	study this afternoon	graduate in May
3. Amir	drive to Los Angeles tomorrow	not fly to Chicago next week
4. Michelle	not play tennis in two hours	watch tennis on TV this weekend
5. Leticia	not go to the pool later	swim at the beach next Saturday
6. Shaza	take an exam later this morning	help her classmates study in a few days

Future Plans Already Made

1. _Linda is visiting her family tonight._

2. _____

3. _____

4. _____

5. _____

6. _____

Future Plans

She isn't going to travel to Paris next week.

_____

_____

_____

_____

_____

4 **A** Write things you or people you know plan to do in the future with *be going to*.

1. I _am going to choose my major_ next year.

2. My best friend _____ in a week or two.

3. My family and I _____ in the future.

4. I _____ next semester.

B Write things you or people you know already planned to do in the future with the present progressive.

1. I _am meeting a friend for dinner_ tonight.

2. My best friend _____ tomorrow.

3. My family and I _____ later today.

4. I _____ on the weekend.

Future with *Will*

1 Complete the sentences about predictions of life 100 years in the future. Use *will* and the base form of the verbs in the boxes.

| build | do | ~~live~~ |
| buy | grow | send |

1. Most people _will live_ in cities.

2. Robots _____ all of the work in factories.

3. Scientists _____ astronauts to other planets.

4. Human beings _____ colonies on the moon.

5. We _____ new foods on the ocean floor.

6. Families _____ everything they need on their cell phones.

be	increase	not drive	not use
find	learn	not go	speak

7. Children _____ to school. They _____ at home with computers.

8. Public transportation _____ fast and cheap. People _____ cars very often.

9. Researchers _____ a cure for cancer.

10. Students _____ any paper.

11. Everyone _____ three or four languages.

12. The world population _____ .

2 Complete the conversation with *will* or *be going to*.

Jack: _I am going to spend_ (be going to: I / spend) a semester in Brazil this fall.
(1)

Sadly, _____ (will: I / not see) any other countries on this trip.
(2)

Alicia: When _____ (will: you / leave)?
(3)

Jack: _____ (be going to: I / leave) on August 26.
(4)

Alicia: What _____ (will: you / do) there?
(5)

Jack: Well, _____ (be going to: I / study) the Brazilian economy and culture,
(6)

and _____ (be going to: I / learn)
(7)

Portuguese.

Alicia: Where _____ (will: you / live)?
(8)

_____ (will: you / stay) with a
(9)

family?

Jack: No, _____ (be going to:
(10)

I / not stay) with a family because

_____ (be going to: I / live) in
(11)

a dorm.

Alicia: Well, have a great time!

3 The sentences below were part of a student's report about homes in the future. Rewrite the sentences with *will* to make them more appropriate for academic writing.

1. Houses are going to be small because the population in cities is going to grow.
   Houses will be small because the population in cities will grow.
2. Houses are not going to have many walls.

   _____

3. Some homes on the coast are going to float on water.

   _____

4. People are not going to use gas or electricity to heat and cool homes.

   _____

5. The sun and wind are going to provide homes with energy.

   _____

6. The materials for building homes are not going to weigh much.

   _____

7. Robots are going to clean our homes.

   _____

8. One computer network is going to control everything in the home.

   _____

4 Write sentences with *will* to make predictions about your life and the lives of your friends and family in the next 10 years. Use the verbs in the box or your own ideas.

apply	do	go	help	meet	sell	speak	study	work

1. *I will speak English very well and I will work as an English teacher.*

2. _____

3. _____

4. _____

5. _____

Avoid Common Mistakes

1 Circle the mistakes.

1. John (**will meet**) with his teacher today at 2 p.m. He **is going to ask for** help, then he
   (a)   (b)
   is going to the library.
   (c)

2. Pat **is going to study** later. Sue **is going to go out** in an hour. I **will write** a paper.
       (a)   (b)   (c)
   Can you help me?

3. In 100 years, energy use **changes**. Gasoline **will not be** common. Solar energy
                            (a)   (b)
   will be common.
   (c)

4. **What you are going to do** when you graduate? **How are you deciding**?
   (a)   (b)
   Where are you going to look for work?
   (c)

5. I **am going to be** an actor. Inna **is going to learn** another language, and her sisters
      (a)   (b)
   going to travel.
   (c)

6. Let's order dinner. **I'm going to have** the chicken. **She's going to take** the fish, and
                        (a)   (b)
   they going to have hamburgers.
   (c)

7. Tony planned his day. First, he **is going to exercise**. Later he **is going to study**, and then
                                    (a)   (b)
   he **going to make** dinner.
   (c)

8. The students **are going to take** an exam. They **going to study** together, and they
                (a)   (b)
   are going to pass it.
   (c)

2 A business owner posted his plans and some questions on an international business blog. Find and correct nine more mistakes.

Community Business Blog

am traveling
I ~~will travel~~ to Berlin tomorrow with my business partner, Mike. We

meeting a possible European business partner the next day. I think we going to

discuss business laws and taxes. What else we are going to talk about? What

information he is going to need from me?

We want to open stores in four cities in Germany, so I going to study German

soon. Can you suggest a good book on business German?

I suppose we encounter some cultural differences. Mike going to do research

on them during our trip. We going to develop a successful business in the next

few years. What else we are going to need to make us successful outside of the

United States?

Self-Assessment

Circle the word or phrase that correctly completes each sentence.

1. Joe is going to work in a college next year. I think his boss _____ the dean.

   a. will be   b. is   c. going to be

2. Tami _____ her class in graphic design tomorrow.

   a. finish   b. finishing   c. is going to finish

3. Carol is busy tonight. She _____ dinner with Jack.

   a. is having   b. going to have   c. will to have

4. I want to use the new library, but it _____ for a few more days.

   a. will not opening   b. will open   c. won't open

5. Finally, my college _____ recycle paper and plastic.

   a. are going to   b. going to   c. is going to

6. _____ at your company? I hear there are big changes.

    a. What happening   b. Is happening   c. What is happening

7. _____ with my class about careers in design?

    a. You will talk   b. Will you talk   c. Talk you

8. The students like their teacher. They _____ another class with her next semester.

    a. going to take   b. are going to take   c. are going take

9. **A:** What would you like to drink? **B:** _____ a coffee, please.

    a. I am going to have   b. I am having   c. I'll have

10. Why _____ Portuguese?

    a. you going to study   b. you are going to study   c. are you going to study

11. I need to go right now, but _____ you tomorrow.

    a. I going to call   b. I am calling   c. I'll call

12. James has plans tonight. _____ his sister.

    a. He's visiting   b. He visiting   c. He going to visit

13. Rita doesn't like her job as a designer. When _____ looking for a new job?

    a. she will start   b. she start   c. will she start

14. In 100 years, we _____ gasoline for cars.

    a. will not use   b. are not using   c. not going to use

15. **A:** Will Paul be in class tomorrow? **B:** No, _____ .

    a. he will   b. he won't   c. he isn't

Will, May, and Might for Future Possibility; Will for Offers and Promises

Will We Need Teachers?

May and Might; Adverbs with Will

1 Complete the sentences with *will*, *may*, or *might*. Sometimes there is more than one correct answer.

1. Pavel <u>*might* OR *may*</u> become a doctor. He isn't sure if his test scores are high enough.

2. Rita _____ start college soon. She is already enrolled in classes at Berk University.

3. Sasha _____ go to her study group tonight. She has two possibilities tonight and can't decide.

4. Anna _____ enroll in night classes. The day classes are already full, so she can't take them.

5. Jae-Hoon _____ visit South Korea next summer. His parents gave him the money to fly home.

6. Tara _____ not buy textbooks for her classes. Her teachers are using all online materials.

7. Zack _____ take nursing classes. He's not certain, but he likes helping sick people.

8. Natalia _____ learn Spanish. Her company is paying for classes.

9. Zena _____ submit her assignment early. She is trying to finish early, but she isn't sure she can.

10. Abdul _____ not pass his math class. He didn't do well on any of his tests.

2 Write sentences about each person using the information in parentheses. Use *will*, *may*, or *might*. Sometimes there is more than one correct answer.

1. Tomás / enroll / in an online math class (100% certain)

    <u>*Tomás will enroll in an online math class.*</u>

2. Linda / write / an article on virtual education (less than 100% certain)

    _____

3. Bill / not study / in the library anymore (100% certain)

    _____

4. Jessica / apply / to law school (less than 100% certain)

    _____

5. Hashi / pass / his class (100% certain)

_____

6. Steve / take / a biology class (less than 100% certain)

_____

7. Mike / ask / the teacher for help (100% certain)

_____

8. Leticia / not learn / Chinese for her job (less than 100% certain)

_____

3 Write sentences about Dr. Bart's engineering class with the information below. Use *will* or *will not* and the adverbs of certainty in parentheses.

1. Dr. Bart / create a website for his engineering class (definitely)

   Dr. Bart will definitely create a website for his engineering class.

2. Many students / use the website (likely)

   _____

3. Students / help Dr. Bart with the website (likely not)

   _____

4. Dr. Bart / put test questions on his website (certainly not)

   _____

5. The final exam / be short (definitely not)

   _____

6. Students who don't study / pass the class (surely not)

   _____

7. The class website / have tips for taking the tests (surely)

   _____

8. Most students / work 20 hours per week to pass the class (possibly)

   _____

Offers and Promises

1 Read the requests on the left and complete the offers on the right. Use *will* / *'ll* and the base form of the verbs.

1. **A:** Can anyone explain this chemistry problem to me?　**B:** ___*I'll explain*___ (I / explain) it to you.

2. **A:** Could someone take Maria to the library?　**B:** _____ (Juan / take) her.

3. **A:** Who will volunteer for the first project?　**B:** _____ (Ann and I / do) it.

4. **A:** Can someone show Jane how to use the software?　**B:** _____ (Minh / show) her.

5. **A:** Can anyone give me the teacher's e-mail address?　**B:** _____ (I / give) it to you.

6. **A:** Would someone lend me a pen?　**B:** _____ (I / lend) you one.

7. **A:** Could someone turn on the lights in the classroom?　**B:** _____ (Jack / turn) them on.

8. **A:** Can someone ask the teacher for a copy of the homework?　**B:** _____ (I / ask) him.

9. **A:** Would anyone like to bring soda to our class potluck?　**B:** _____ (Lan and Tina / bring) some.

10. **A:** Could someone tell Amir we changed our study group time?　**B:** _____ (I / tell) him.

2 Complete the conversation. Use the offers and promises in the boxes. Add *I'll* or *I won't*.

Offers
~~lend you my notes~~
come to get you at 3:00 p.m.
join you

Promises
not forget
return them tomorrow
take you to my house for dinner with my family
arrive on time

Andy: I lost my class notes. I need to borrow them from someone in our class.

Miguel: ___*I'll lend you my notes.*___
(1)

Andy: That's great! _____ .
(2)

Miguel: Don't forget! I'll need them for class.

Andy: I promise. _____ .
(3)

Miguel: By the way, my friends and I are playing soccer tomorrow, and we need a few more players.

Andy: _____ . I'd love to play.
(4)

Miguel: OK. _____ , and we'll go to the park
$\quad$ (5)

around 3:30 p.m.

Andy: Perfect! After the game _____ .
$\quad\qquad$ (6)

My family loves it when I bring guests. Just remember to be on time.

Miguel: Sounds good to me. _____ .
$\quad\qquad$ (7)

3 Read Sandra's requests and complete the promises she makes. Use *will* or *won't* and the base form of the verbs.

1. Can I borrow your computer? <u>*I won't break it*</u>
   (I / not break).

2. Could you help me with my work? _____
   (I / help) you next time.

3. Can Maria use your cell phone? _____
   (she / be) careful.

4. Could Tim take your workbook home tonight?

   _____ (he / not write) in it.

5. Can I make a copy of your class notes? _____
   (I / give) them back in 10 minutes.

6. Could you get the coffee for us? _____ (I / take) your books to class.

7. Can they do their class presentation first? _____ (they / let) you do
   yours first next time.

8. Could you buy Jorge a notebook? _____ (he / pay) you back later.

9. Can you send me an e-mail? _____ (I / read) it and answer you.

10. Could Mark and Sue see your answers? _____ (they / not show)
    them to anyone.

4 A Write offers with *will* to respond to these statements.

1. **A:** I don't know how to use this DVD player.

   B: *I'll show you how to use it.* OR *I'll help you with it.*

2. **A:** I'm hungry.

   B: _____

3. **A:** I don't want to be late for work.

   B: _____

4. **A:** I'm cold.

   B: _____

B Read the requests below. Write promises based on those requests.

1. Can I use your laptop? *I won't break it.*

2. Could I borrow your camera? _____

3. Can I work with you on the group project? _____

4. Could I see your essay? _____

5. Can I borrow your notes from class? _____

6. Could I ask you a question? _____

7. Can I have a ride home? _____

8. Could I use your phone? _____

Avoid Common Mistakes

1 Circle the mistakes.

1. Schools definitely (can) change soon. We **may** not have teachers, and we **might** not
   (a)   (b)   (c)
   have classrooms.

2. Virtual classrooms **will use** the Internet. **May be** you **will** take all your courses
                        (a)   (b)   (c)
   from home.

3. There **will be** virtual language labs. Textbooks **might be** digital, and all homework
              (a)   (b)
   maybe online.
     (c)

4. Tests **might become** interactive. Students **can create** their tests, and teachers
    (a)   (b)

   might not grade them.
   (c)

5. In 50 years, libraries **may disappear**. **May be** all libraries **will be** digital.
   (a)   (b)   (c)

6. Some day, all colleges **may be** free. **Maybe** students **can** not pay tuition.
   (a)   (b)   (c)

7. Students **can** be able to travel in space. **Maybe** they **will** visit other planets and meet
   (a)   (b)   (c)
   new life forms.

8. Students **may text** their teachers. **Maybe** all contact with teachers **can be** online.
   (a)   (b)   (c)

2 Find and correct eight more mistakes in this student's opinion article from a school newspaper.

> ### Here are eight possible changes I see for education in the next 50 years:
>
> 1. We probably ~~can~~ *will* not use cash or checks at school. All financial exchanges maybe electronic.
>
> 2. Schools might not have semesters. Students can be able to start and end a class when they want.
>
> 3. May be all study groups for students will be online.
>
> 4. All students can definitely have to take classes in science and technology.
>
> 5. All students maybe required to speak and write in two languages.
>
> 6. Students can surely choose their teachers from any country in the world.
>
> 7. Schools might not need classrooms. They can stop constructing buildings.
>
> 8. High schools and colleges can not be separate. They may be one institution.
>
> We should get ready to learn in new ways. It's already starting!

Self-Assessment

Circle the word or phrase that correctly completes each sentence.

1. I definitely _____ take a math class next semester.

    a. will not   b. might not   c. may be

2. If you help me with my homework, _____ definitely take you home.

    a. I may   b. I'll   c. I

3. Students _____ teachers in the future.

    a. probably won't need   b. won't probably need   c. won't need probably

4. E-books _____ more popular than paper books in 10 years.

    a. maybe   b. may be   c. maybe will

5. Library buildings _____ in the future.

    a. maybe close   b. might close   c. can close

6. Professor Nguyen _____ his best to help his students.

    a. will do certainly   b. do certainly will   c. will certainly do

7. I need my class notes today. _____ them to you tomorrow.

    a. I lend   b. I'll lend   c. I'll can lend

8. _____ all classes be online in the future?

    a. Will   b. May   c. Do

9. Some classes _____ online in the future.

    a. mightn't be   b. mayn't be   c. might not be

10. _____ all teachers will teach online.

    a. May be   b. Maybe   c. May be can

11. **A:** Are you going on the virtual field trip this week? **B:** _____ .

    a. I might   b. I can   c. I do

12. I am sure that I _____ not go to class tomorrow.

    a. will   b. may   c. might

13. Colleges _____ more online classes in the next five years.

    a. will not surely offer   b. will surely offer   c. will offer surely

14. Students _____ to take notes in the future.

    a. cannot need   b. will not need   c. will cannot need

15. In two years, _____ the school offer this class in two or three languages?

    a. may   b. will   c. might not

Suggestions and Advice

Study Habits

Modals for Suggestions and Advice

1 Rewrite this list of study strategies. Use the words given to make suggestions.

Quick Tips for Success in College

1. Review your notes before going to class.

(you / should) *You should review your notes before going to class.*

2. Don't miss class.

(you / should not) _____

3. Create a weekly schedule.

(you / might want to) _____

4. Concentrate on finishing tasks on time.

(you / might want to) _____

5. Ask a teacher for help.

(you / should) _____

6. Don't stay awake all night before a test.

(you / might not want to) _____

7. Join a study group.

(you / ought to) _____

8. Don't get distracted by TV or video games.

(you / should not) _____

2 Give suggestions for each situation. Write the same suggestion two ways. Use the modals given and the bold words to help you.

1. Robert is failing his math class. He never **studies**.

    should   _He should study._

    might want to   _He might want to study._

2. Tina and John cannot attend their English class tomorrow. They don't **inform their professor**.

    might want to   _____

    ought to   _____

3. Some students fall asleep in their morning classes. They **stay up late at night**.

    might not want to   _____

    should not   _____

4. I need to prepare for a test tomorrow. I am **going to a movie tonight**.

    should not   _____

    might not want to   _____

5. Juan wants to improve his note taking. He doesn't **pay attention to the teacher**.

    should   _____

    might want to   _____

6. John always arrives late to his classes. He **leaves his house just before class begins**.

    might not want to   _____

    should not   _____

3 Complete the conversations between students. Use *Let's (not) . . .* and *Why don't you / we . . . ?* Look at the end punctuation when choosing your answers.

1. **A:** I need some help with my homework. Can you help me?

    B: Sure, _let's meet_ (we / meet) in the library at 6:00 p.m., and we can work on it then.

2. **A:** We never have enough time to study for our tests.

    B: That's true. _Why don't we create_ (we / create) a study schedule next time and try to follow it?

3. **A:** Sometimes my friends and I can't find a place to study.

   B: _____ (you / reserve) a study room in the library once a week?

4. **A:** I want to improve my vocabulary. I need some new strategies.

   B: _____ (you / use) a dictionary when you find a word you don't understand?

5. **A:** We can start our class project in a few days. We still have time.

   B: No, _____ (we / not wait). It might take us a few days to complete it.

6. **A:** We study every day for hours and hours. Don't you get tired?

   B: Yeah, sometimes. _____ (we / take) a break and go to a movie tonight?

7. **A:** It's not easy to take notes in class. Our teacher talks fast.

   B: _____ (you / bring) a tape recorder to class and record the lecture? You can listen later.

8. **A:** I'd like to take Dr. Pace's economics class next semester. They say she is a great teacher.

   B: I heard that, too. _____ (we / register) for her class soon before it fills up.

Asking for and Responding to Suggestions and Advice

1 Write *Yes / No* questions asking for advice. Then choose responses from the box.

| Absolutely! | I'm not sure. | Probably. | That sounds great! |
| ~~Definitely!~~ | Maybe. | That's not a good idea. | Why don't you wait until next year? |

1. I / review / the chapters assigned for homework

   Q: *Should I review the chapters assigned for homework?*   **A:** *Definitely!*
   (strong positive)

2. we / take / a short break

   Q: _____   **A:** _____
   (no)

3. we / turn off / the music

   Q: _____   **A:** _____
   (uncertain)

4. I / choose / a major this semester

   Q: _____   **A:** _____
   (no)

5. I / join / your study group

   Q: _____   A: _____
                                                          (strong positive)

6. we / arrive / early for the test

   Q: _____   A: _____
                                                          (uncertain)

7. we / create / note cards to help us

   Q: _____   A: _____
                                                          (strong positive)

8. I / call / my teacher

   Q: _____   A: _____
                                                          (uncertain)

2 Write information questions using *should* and the words in parentheses.

1. **Q:** (Where / I / study) *Where should I study tonight?* _____

   A: You should study in the library.

2. **Q:** (When / we / start studying) _____

   A: We should start studying at 3:00 p.m.

3. **Q:** (Who / I / ask for help) _____

   A: You should ask your teacher for help.

4. **Q:** (What / we / create) _____

   A: You should create practice questions for the test.

5. **Q:** (Why / we / study hard) _____

   A: You should study hard because you need good grades.

6. **Q:** (What / we / bring for the math test) _____

   A: You should bring a calculator and a pencil for the math test.

7. **Q:** (What / I / eat / before the test) _____

   A: You should eat a good breakfast before the test.

8. **Q:** (Where / we / meet / tomorrow afternoon) _____

   A: We should meet at the library tomorrow afternoon.

3 Use the rules in the flyer to help you complete the conversation between the students. Use *should* in the questions and answers.

Rules for Reserving Study Rooms in the Library

- No more than five students in a room.
- Reserve a room two days in advance.
- Speak to a librarian to reserve a room.
- Bring laptops to use Wi-Fi connection.
- Rooms not open in the morning.

Cheng: Hi Ramón. Let's reserve a study room at the library to prepare for our exam.

Ramón: _How many students should we invite_ (how many / students / we / invite)?
(1)

Cheng: _We should have no more than five students_ (we / have no more …).
(2)

Ramón: _____ (when / we / reserve the room)?
(3)

Cheng: _____ (we / reserve it …).
(4)

Ramón: _____ (we / bring our laptops)?
(5)

Cheng: Yes, _____ (we / bring). The rooms have Wi-Fi.
(6)

Ramón: _____ (who / we / speak with) to reserve a room?
(7)

Cheng: _____ (we / speak with …).
(8)

Ramón: _____ (we / study in the morning)?
(9)

Cheng: No, _____ (we / not study) then. The rooms aren't open.
(10)

Ramón: OK. Let's reserve a room for tomorrow afternoon.

Avoid Common Mistakes

1 Circle the mistakes.

1. **A:** When **should I study**? **B:** You (should to study) later. You **might want to try** the morning.
   (a)   (b)   (c)

2. Oscar **should not probably work** late. He **should study** after work, and he
   (a)   (b)

   ought to review his notes.
   (c)

3. Sandra **should not text** her professor. She **ought send** an e-mail, and she
   (a)   (b)

   should write clearly.
   (c)

4. We **should not bother** the teacher now. We **ought see** a tutor. Or we **should call**
    (a)   (b)   (c)

   another classmate.

5. You **should make** an outline. You **ought to probably underline** ideas.
    (a)   (b)

   You **might want to take notes**.
              (c)

6. You **should study** early. You **ought to** create a practice test, and you
    (a)   (b)

   should not probably stay up late.
       (c)

7. Where **should we meet** to study? What **we should do** first? Who **should we invite** to
          (a)   (b)   (c)

   study with us?

8. Bill **should plans** a study schedule. He **should go** to all his classes, and he
        (a)   (b)

   should not be late.
        (c)

2 Three students are chatting online about their group project. Find and correct the mistakes.

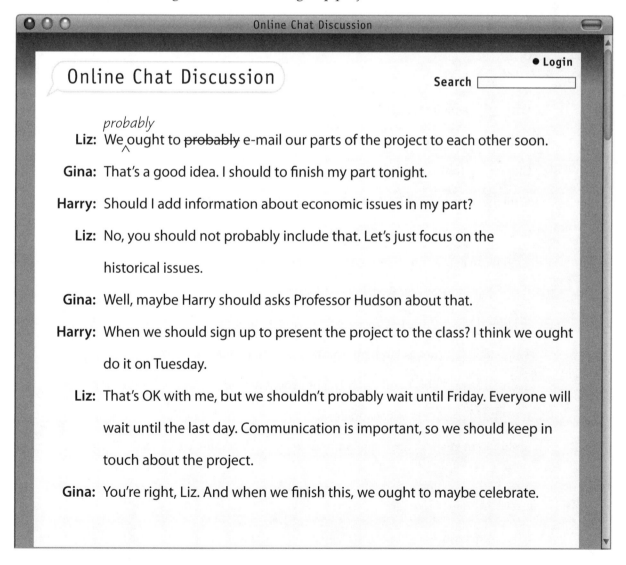

○ ○ ○   Online Chat Discussion

Online Chat Discussion   ● Login

                                     Search [   ]

                probably
Liz: We ˄ought to ~~probably~~ e-mail our parts of the project to each other soon.

Gina: That's a good idea. I should to finish my part tonight.

Harry: Should I add information about economic issues in my part?

Liz: No, you should not probably include that. Let's just focus on the

   historical issues.

Gina: Well, maybe Harry should asks Professor Hudson about that.

Harry: When we should sign up to present the project to the class? I think we ought

   do it on Tuesday.

Liz: That's OK with me, but we shouldn't probably wait until Friday. Everyone will

   wait until the last day. Communication is important, so we should keep in

   touch about the project.

Gina: You're right, Liz. And when we finish this, we ought to maybe celebrate.

Self-Assessment

Circle the word or phrase that correctly completes each sentence.

1. You _____ get eight hours of sleep before your test.

   a. should to   b. might want to   c. ought

2. Are you busy tonight? Let's _____ together and study.

   a. to get   b. getting   c. get

3. _____ a study schedule this week?

   a. I should to plan   b. Should I plan   c. Should I planning

4. Why _____ at the school café after class?

   a. we don't stop   b. don't he stops   c. don't we stop

5. Joey _____ his classes.

   a. might not want to miss   b. might not want miss   c. might to want to go

6. **A:** Should I check the class website? **B:** _____ .

   a. No, you don't   b. Yes, he might   c. That's a good idea

7. Why _____ a biology class?

   a. they should take   b. should they take   c. should they to take

8. Chen _____ to this part of the lecture again.

   a. might want listen   b. might wants to listen   c. might want to listen

9. Jason _____ lunch before he studies.

   a. ought to eat   b. ought eat   c. ought to eats

10. _____ the chemistry class. It's very difficult.

    a. Let not take   b. Let's not take   c. Let's not to take

11. Students _____ the research on how to study more effectively.

    a. ought to probably read   b. ought probably read   c. probably ought to read

12. I _____ a journal of new vocabulary words.

    a. should to keep   b. might want to keep   c. ought keep

13. Erin _____ out before she finishes her homework.

   a. probably should not go   b. should not probably go   c. ought probably not go

14. **A:** Why don't we study later? **B:** _____ .

   a. I don't   b. I can't   c. I'm not

15. Kyle _____ on his study goals.

   a. should focuses   b. ought to focuses   c. should focus

Necessity and Conclusions

Getting What You Want

Necessity and Conclusions with *Have To, Need To, Must*

1 Isabel just got engaged to be married. Read the list of things she must do before the wedding. Decide whether each thing is necessary, not necessary, or forbidden.

	Necessary	Not Necessary	Forbidden
1. Isabel needs to choose a location for the wedding.	✓		
2. She and her mother must shop for a wedding dress.			
3. They don't need to order many flowers.			
4. She must not show the wedding dress to the groom.[1]			
5. She has to decide what food to serve.			
6. She doesn't have to have a live band.			

---

[1] **groom:** man that the bride marries

2 Complete the conversation with (*not*) *have to*, (*not*) *need to*, and *must* (*not*).

Amal: Hi, Diego. You studied in London last semester, right? When is the enrollment deadline?

Diego: You *don't need to enroll* (not need to / enroll) in the program until August.
(1)

Amal: OK, but I _____ (have to / apply) for a passport. I
(2)

don't have one. Can you help me?

Diego: Sure. Since this is your first passport, you

_____ (must / apply) in
(3)

person. You _____ (not have to
(4)

/ go) to a passport agency. You can just go to a post office.

Amal: Great. What do I need to take with me?

Diego: You _____ (need to / download) the passport application
     (5)

from the government website. Also, you _____
                                                  (6)

(must / bring) your birth certificate and a current ID card. You

_____ (must not / forget) to bring two pictures of
     (7)

yourself. You _____ (have to / go) to a special passport
                              (8)

photo place for that.

Amal: All right. I can do that. Anything else?

Diego: You _____ (need to / pay) for the application. You
                        (9)

_____ (not need to / take) cash. They accept credit
        (10)

cards, checks, and money orders, too.

Amal: Great! I'll apply at the post office this week, then. Thanks, Diego!

3 Write *Yes / No* or information questions with *have to* or *need to* about using the school gym.

1. when / members / leave (have to)

   A: *When do members have to leave?* _____

   B: They have to leave by 10:00 p.m.

2. you / bring a towel (need to)

   A: _____

   B: No, you don't need to bring a towel.

3. members / wear gym shoes (have to)

   A: _____

   B: Yes, members have to wear gym shoes.

4. what / members / bring to the yoga classes (have to)

   A: _____

   B: They have to bring a yoga mat.

5. you / carry / your gym ID (need to)

   A: _____

   B: Yes, you need to carry your gym ID.

6. where / members / show their gym ID (have to)

   A: _____

   B: They have to show their ID at the front desk.

7. you / use the pool (have to)

A: _____

B: No, you do not have to use the pool.

8. where / you / put your personal items (have to)

A: _____

B: You have to put them in a locker.

4 Complete the short conversations. Use a verb of necessity or conclusion with the words in parentheses. Sometimes there is more than one correct answer.

A   **Bob:** Hi Jim, what are you doing at my gym? You _____*must be*_____ (be) a member
                                        (1)
              here, too.

    Jim: Yeah, I _____ (lose) weight, so I joined this gym.
                        (2)

B   **Mike:** Hey, Tanya. I received my final grade for Biology 202. I got an "A"!

   Tanya: That's great. You _____ (feel) very proud. I _____
                                    (3)   (4)
              (take) that class soon.

C   **Joe:** Daniela, did you just get home from work?

 Daniela: Yes. On Mondays and Wednesdays I _____ (work) for 12 hours.
                                            (5)

     Joe: You _____ (be) very tired. I'm glad you _____
                           (6)   (7)
              (not / do) anything else tonight. Just rest.

D   **Eric:** I went to another concert last night. I really _____ (start) saving
                                          (8)
              my money.

    Jess: You _____ (love) music! You sure do buy a lot of tickets. You
                         (9)
              _____ (have) a lot of extra money to spend!
               (10)

E   **Yulia:** Claudia, your parents are from Italy, right? You _____ (speak) Italian.
                                                (11)

 Claudia: I can speak Italian OK, but I _____ (take) a class so I can learn to
                                        (12)
              write it.

Avoid Common Mistakes

1 Circle the mistakes.

1. Cathy **has to open** the office. She **needs to supervise** employees, and she

(a) (b)
   (must to write) reports.

(c)

2. Pedro **doesn't need to see** an adviser. He **must submit** an application, and he

(a) (b)
   has to sends a transcript.

(c)

3. **A:** Does Sandy **has to take** the class again? **B:** Yes, she **needs to study** more, and she

(a) (b)
   must not be late.

(c)

4. My friends **have to read** more. They **need to get** a tutor. They **has to practice** writing every day.

(a) (b) (c)

5. **A:** Do you **need to get** a driver's license? **B:** Yes, I **have to complete** a course, and I

(a) (b)
   must to take a test.

(c)

6. Juan **needs to choose** a career. He **doesn't has to network**, but he **must not wait** to start looking.

(a) (b) (c)

7. Eva **needs to exercise**. She **has to buy** healthy food, and she **must eats** fewer calories.

(a) (b) (c)

8. You didn't eat today. You **need to be** hungry. You **need to buy** lunch. You

(a) (b)
   need to eat regularly.

(c)

2 Read the interview with a 75-year-old woman who finished a marathon. Find and correct eight more mistakes.

Run Fast Magazine

Interviewer: Congratulations on finishing the marathon yesterday. You ~~needs to~~ *must* be exhausted.

Elena: Yes, I do feel tired, but I'll get some rest. I must to work hard to run a marathon. But at the age of 75, I still feel great and hope to run a marathon next year, too.

Interviewer: You need to have many tips for runners. Tell us what someone has to does to train for a marathon at your age.

Elena: Well, you has to like running, and you must to develop a plan that will help you reach your goal.

Interviewer: Does a person in training needs to run every day?

Elena: No, you don't has to run every day, but you need to run at least four to five times a week. Persistence is very important!

Interviewer: Well, you must to feel proud. Get some rest!

Self-Assessment

Circle the word or phrase that correctly completes each sentence.

1. When _____ need to apply for a grant?

   a. do you   b. does you   c. you

2. Tao is from Beijing. He _____ how to speak Chinese.

   a. must knows   b. must to know   c. must know

3. The students _____ prepare for their exam.

   a. needs to   b. have to   c. must to

4. A student _____ late for class.

    a. must not arrives   b. don't have to arrive   c. must not arrive

5. Peter _____ complete his assignment by tomorrow.

    a. need to   b. doesn't need to   c. have to

6. Does Leticia _____ tonight?

    a. need to studies   b. needs to study   c. need to study

7. Ruth and Rick have very good grades. They _____ be intelligent.

    a. must   b. need to   c. has to

8. **A:** Do the students have to apply for the scholarship? **B:** Yes, they _____ .

    a. are   b. can   c. do

9. What _____ to do to lower their education costs?

    a. has they   b. do they have   c. they have

10. Applicants _____ be persistent when they apply for a grant.

    a. must   b. should to   c. must to

11. A runner _____ a specific training schedule to run a marathon.

    a. have to follow   b. must follow   c. need to follows

12. I _____ to create a study schedule that is appropriate for me.

    a. needs   b. have   c. must

13. How old _____ to drive in this state?

    a. do you have to be   b. have to be   c. must you have

14. Teachers _____ available to help students outside of the classroom.

    a. has to be   b. need to be   c. need to are

15. Do you _____ ambition to be a good student?

    a. have to have   b. has to have   c. have to has

UNIT 31

Adjectives and Adverbs
Making a Good Impression

Adjectives and Adverbs of Manner

1 Write the adjective or adverb form of the words in parentheses to complete the conversation.

David: Hi, Kate. I hear you started class with Dr. Smith.

He is a (strict)/ **strictly** instructor, but he explains
$\quad$ (1)
his material **clear / clearly**. You can make a
$\quad$ (2)
good / well impression on him by doing a few
$\quad$ (3)
simple / simply things.
$\quad$ (4)

Kate: Great. Please tell me. I already showed him I'm a

serious / seriously student. I submitted my first
$\quad$ (5)
report early.

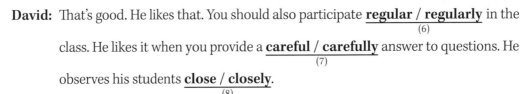

David: That's good. He likes that. You should also participate **regular / regularly** in the
$\qquad\qquad\qquad\qquad\qquad\qquad\qquad\qquad\qquad\qquad\qquad$ (6)
class. He likes it when you provide a **careful / carefully** answer to questions. He
$\qquad\qquad\qquad\qquad\qquad\qquad\qquad$ (7)
observes his students **close / closely**.
$\qquad\qquad\qquad\qquad\qquad\qquad$ (8)

Kate: Yesterday, Dr. Smith explained about plagiarism, and he taught us to cite our

sources **correct / correctly**. He also showed us how to organize our papers
$\qquad\qquad\qquad$ (9)
effective / effectively.
$\quad$ (10)

David: Good. Well, everything we discussed will help you make a good impression. He

has an **excellent / excellently** class. I know you will **total / totally** enjoy it.
$\qquad\qquad$ (11) $\qquad\qquad\qquad\qquad\qquad\qquad\qquad\qquad\qquad$ (12)

2 Complete the conversations below. Use the adjective and adverb forms of the words given.

1. good   **A:** I'm meeting Jorge's family tomorrow and want to make a

                  good impression.

      B: Great! Remember to present yourself _well_ .

2. slow   **A:** Hermosa is learning English, and she speaks _____ .

      B: Learning English can be a _____ process. Be patient[1] with her.

3. careful   **A:** If you do your work _____ , your boss will notice.

      B: I know. I am very _____ with my work and my boss was impressed.

4. loud   **A:** My neighbors were playing their music _____ yesterday.

      B: _____ music bothers my mother.

5. different   **A:** Did you notice that Ryan talks _____ from the other students?

      B: Yes. He has a _____ accent. It's not like ours. He's from New Zealand.

6. easy   **A:** This class is _____ . I'm sure I'll get a good grade.

      B: I agree. I think all the students in class will pass _____ .

7. automatic   **A:** In new situations, people should say please and thank you

                  _____ .

      B: Yes. It needs to be an _____ response. It's important to be polite.

8. quick   **A:** I know you don't have much time. Here's a _____ recipe you can use to impress your dinner guests tonight.

      B: Perfect. I need something I can prepare _____ . I'm very busy today.

9. early   **A:** Jim must want to impress his teacher. He submits his assignments

                  _____ .

      B: Why? My assignments are never _____ , but they're on time. I still do well.

10. hard   **A:** Learning a new language is _____ .

      B: You're right. I study _____ every day, but I still don't speak very well.

---

[1]**patient:** able to wait without complaining, or not easily annoyed

3 A doctor wants to make a good impression on his new patients. Write sentences with the adverb or adjective form of the underlined words and the words in parentheses. Write the adverb form when the adjective is given. Write the adjective form when the adverb is given.

1. He has a **gentle** voice.

   He speaks gently.
   (he / speak)

2. His clothes are **neat**.

   _____
   (he / dress)

3. He **clearly** answers questions.

   _____
   (he / be / with his staff)

4. He has a lot of **good** information about his patients.[1]

   _____
   (he / know / his patients)

5. He speaks with his patients **honestly**.

   _____
   (he / be)

6. He **generously** shares his time.

   _____
   (he / be)

7. He is a **careful** listener.

   _____
   (he / listen)

8. He is **respectful** when he talks with patients.

   _____
   (he / talk)

9. He advises patients **effectively**.

   _____
   (he / give / advice)

10. He is **early** for his appointments.

    _____
    (he / arrive)

[1]**patient:** person who receives medical care

4 Write sentences about the important qualities of the people below. Use the adjectives and adverbs in the box or your own ideas.

careful	clear	gentle	immediately	quickly
carefully	friendly	happy	properly	well

1. A good doctor _A good doctor contacts her patients immediately when she receives lab results._

2. A good teacher _____

3. A good employee _____

4. A good student _____

5. A good nurse _____

6. A good mechanic _____

7. A good friend _____

8. A good child _____

Adjectives with Linking Verbs; Adjectives and Adverbs with *Very* and *Too*

1 Susan tried to make a good impression on her dinner guests. Write the adjective or adverb form of the words in parentheses.

1. Susan wanted her house to look **nice** / **nicely**. She spent a whole week cleaning it.

2. She wanted the food to taste **good** / **well**. She bought fresh ingredients.

3. Her husband got **nervous** / **nervously**, so he drank a lot of water.

4. The dinner smelled **wonderful** / **wonderfully**.

5. Her son began practicing his guitar in his room. It sounded **loud** / **loudly** to the guests.

6. Susan spoke to him and he started playing **quiet** / **quietly**.

7. The food was delicious, and all the guests ate **happily** / **happy**.

8. The dinner party was a success because of Susan's **careful** / **carefully** plans for the evening.

2 Use the pictures to describe Julia's first day in a new office. Write sentences with *too* or *very* and the words below.

1. the box / heavy

   The box is too heavy.

2. the office supplies / high

   _____

3. the desk / small

   _____

4. Julia's boss / speak / quickly

   _____

5. Julia / arrived / early

   _____

3 Complete each sentence with *too* + adjective or adverb + infinitive.

1. My last assignment was easy, but this assignment is *too difficult to finish* (difficult / finish).

2. This book is interesting, but that book is _____ (boring / read).

3. The speaker is confident, but her business partner is _____ (shy / give) a presentation.

4. Lina registered for the class early, but Rick is _____ (late / register).

5. Ying is tall, and Mark is _____ (short / wear) Ying's jacket.

6. Robert speaks slowly, but Nancy speaks _____ (quickly / understand).

7. Asad wasn't feeling well. He left the party _____ (early / have) any cake.

8. Tania's cooking tastes good, but Jordy's cooking tastes _____ (bad / eat).

9. Jawad's new car is great. His old car is _____ (old / drive).

10. Let's go to the library. It is _____ (noisy / study) in the student lounge.

11. Sandra was not on time. She arrived _____ (late / take) the test.

12. The movie had subtitles, but they moved _____ (fast / read).

Avoid Common Mistakes

1 Circle the mistakes.

1. The woman **seemed friendly**. She **looked confidently**, and she **dressed nicely**.
   (a)   (b)   (c)

2. The speaker presented the information **good**. The audience didn't get **bored**, and they
                                          (a)   (b)
   clapped **loudly**.
           (c)

3. The teacher **prepared the test carefully**, **gave clearly instructions**, and
                (a)   (b)
   graded the test fairly.
   (c)

4. In order to get a **good grade** in this course, you should **study hardly** and **arrive early** to class.
                     (a)   (b)   (c)

5. In order to impress your teacher, **listen carefully**, **smile warmly**, and
                                     (a)   (b)
   submit regularly homework.
   (c)

6. When Mary meets new people, she **gets nervously**, **seems uncomfortable**, and **feels afraid**.
                                   (a)   (b)   (c)

7. The students **studied hard**, **prepared good** for the test, and made a **good impression**
                (a)   (b)   (c)
   on their teacher.

8. A good boss is **too helpful**, **listens well**, and provides **good directions**.
                  (a)   (b)   (c)

2 Alexis wrote to an online advice column. Find and correct the mistakes.

Manners Blog   Search [＿＿＿＿＿＿＿＿＿]

Alexis: My family and I just moved into a new neighborhood. We want to

make a ~~well~~ *good* impression on our neighbors. The problem is that my children get

quietly around new people and don't want to talk. My husband is too kind,

and people like him, but he doesn't seem confident with people he doesn't

know good. And when I get nervously, I talk too fast. Can you help us?

MannersGuru: Your family sounds too nice. First, tell your children it's OK to

be shy in new situations. Tell your husband to shake firmly hands and smile

happy when he greets others. You also need to speak slow. Relax and enjoy

meeting your new neighbors.

Self-Assessment

Circle the word or phrase that correctly completes each sentence.

1. The teacher talks _____ .

   a. loudly   b. friendly   c. lively

2. Karl can speak _____ .

   a. fluently German   b. German fluently   c. German fluent

3. Rita cleaned _____ .

   a. her room complete   b. her room completely   c. completely her room

4. The experience of giving a presentation was _____ repeat.

   a. very scary for   b. too scary for   c. too scary to

5. The doctor treats his patients _____ .

   a. respectful   b. respectfully   c. lovely

6. James studies by himself often. Sometimes he gets _____ .

   a. lonely   b. alone   c. lone

7. The boy ran _____ and impressed his coach.

    a. fastly   b. quick   c. fast

8. When he left his country, he missed his family _____ .

    a. terriblely   b. terrible   c. terribly

9. Sonia wore a lovely dress to the party. She looked _____ .

    a. beautifully   b. beautiful   c. nicely

10. Abdul drove fast. I was in his car, and I was afraid. He drove _____ .

    a. too quickly   b. very quick   c. too quick

11. Raj ate _____ .

    a. slowly his dinner   b. his dinner slowly   c. his dinner slow

12. I get _____ when I meet new people.

    a. nervously   b. too nervously   c. nervous

13. Sarah has a _____ .

    a. boss helpful   b. helpfully boss   c. helpful boss

14. The music was _____ study.

    a. too loud   b. too loudly to   c. too loud to

15. When Kenji was nervous he took _____ .

    a. deep breaths   b. deeply breaths   c. breaths deep

UNIT 32

Comparative Adjectives and Adverbs

Progress

Comparative Adjectives

1 Complete the sentences about recent changes in New York City with comparative adjectives. Use the words in parentheses. With ↑ use *more* and with ↓ use *less*.

1. The city is _*more crowded*_ (↑ crowded) than before.

2. Tourists feel _____ (↑ comfortable) in most parts of the city now than in the past.

3. It's also _____ (↓ difficult) to navigate than many tourists think.

4. Today, subway cars are _____ (↓ hot) than in the past.

5. Driving in the city is _____ (↓ convenient) than a ride on the subway.

6. The subway system is _____ (↑ big) than most others.

2 A local newspaper published an article about how the Main Street Restaurant has changed since 2007. Complete the sentences with comparative adjectives. Use the words in parentheses.

1. The menu in 2007 was small. Today, the restaurant has a _*bigger menu*_ (big / menu).

2. In 2007, the hours of operation were short. Today, the restaurant has

_____ (long / hours).

3. The drinks in 2007 were not expensive. Today, the restaurant serves

_____ (expensive / drinks).

4. In 2007, the tables were small. Today, the restaurant has _____
(large / tables).

5. The food in 2007 was not nutritious. Today, the restaurant has

_____ (nutritious / food).

6. In 2007, the customers were senior citizens. Today, the restaurant has

_____ (young / customers).

7. The music in the restaurant in 2007 was loud. Today, the restaurant plays

_____ (soft / music).

8. In 2007, the location was not convenient. Today, the restaurant has a

_____ (convenient / location).

9. The service in 2007 was not good. Today, the restaurant has _____
(good / service).

10. In 2007, the atmosphere was not friendly. Today, the restaurant has a

_____ (friendly / atmosphere).

11. The parking in 2007 was far away. Today the restaurant has _____
(close / parking).

3 Look at the information about the Empire State Building and the Burj Khalifa Tower. Use
the facts to write sentences comparing the two buildings. Use the comparative form of the
adjectives below and *than*.

Empire State Building (New York)

- 1,250 feet tall
- Completed in 1931
- Cost to build: $41 million
- Weight: 340,000 tons
- Architecture: Art Deco

Burj Khalifa Tower (Dubai)

- 2,717 feet tall
- Completed in 2010
- Cost to build: $1.5 billion
- Weight: 500,000 tons
- Architecture: Modern

1. short   _The Empire State Building is shorter than the Burj Khalifa Tower._

2. tall   _____

3. old   _____

4. new   _____

5. cheap   _____

6. expensive   _____

7. light   _____

8. heavy   _____

4 Write sentences using comparative adjectives and *than* about two cities or countries you know. Use the nouns given. Use the comparative form of the adjectives from the box or your own ideas.

cheap	~~efficient~~	happy
good	expensive	interesting

1. public transportation

   San Francisco has more efficient public transportation than Los Angeles.

2. people

_____

3. shopping

_____

4. students

_____

5. food

_____

6. housing

_____

Comparative Adverbs

1 Paul was in the hospital last week for surgery. This week, he is home. Compare his condition last week to his condition this week. Use the comparative form of the adverbs in parentheses.

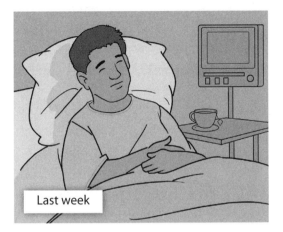
Last week

This week

1. Paul is feeling _better_ (well) this week.

2. Paul was moving _____ (slowly) last week.

3. He is moving _____ (quickly) this week.

4. He was waking up _____ (late) last week.

5. He is getting up _____ (early) this week.

6. Paul is eating _____ (frequently) this week.

7. He was sleeping _____ (lightly) last week.

8. He is sleeping _____ (deeply) this week.

9. His medicines are working _____ (effectively) this week.

10. He was talking _____ (softly) last week.

11. He is speaking _____ (normally) this week.

2 Complete the list of changes the world went through from the twentieth century to the twenty-first century. Use the comparative form of the adverb and the words below. With ↑ use *more* and with ↓ use *less*.

1. people / dressed / formal (↓)

    People dressed less formally for work 50 years ago than they do today.

2. cars / run / efficiently (↑)

    Cars run more efficiently today than in the 1980s.

3. families / live / simply (↓)

    _____ today than in the 1940s.

4. planes / flew / frequently (↓)

_____ in the 1950s than they do today.

5. products / sell / successfully (↑)

_____ on the Internet today than in the 1990s.

6. people / behave / respectfully (↓)

_____ today than in the 1960s.

7. technology / advances / rapidly (↑)

_____ today than in the twentieth century.

8. medicine / works / effectively (↑)

_____ today than 30 years ago.

9. people / traveled / often (↓)

_____ in the 1960s than they do today.

10. people / eat / carefully (↑)

_____ today than 30 years ago.

3 Jane and Eun-Sook work in the same office. Complete the sentences with the comparative form of the adverbs from the box and *than*.

calmly	clearly	efficiently	late
carefully	early	frequently	~~quickly~~

1. Eun-Sook works _more quickly than_ Jane. She gets a lot done in little time.

2. Jane serves customers _____ Eun-Sook. Her customers appreciate her efficient work.

3. Eun-Sook completes her assignments _____ Jane. She is careful with everything she does.

4. Jane uses the copy machine _____ Eun-Sook. Her boss often asks her to make copies.

5. Eun-Sook speaks on the phone _____ Jane. Her voice is clear and easy to understand.

6. Jane begins her workday _____ Eun-Sook. She arrives at the office at 7:00 a.m., and Eun-Sook arrives at 10:00 a.m.

7. Eun-Sook starts her day _____ Jane. She gets to work at 10:00 a.m., and Jane gets there at 7:00 a.m.

8. Jane handles office problems _____ Eun-Sook. She never gets upset or nervous.

4 People and places change over time. Write sentences about people or places you know that have changed in the past few years. Use the comparative form of the adverbs.

1. frequently   *My best friend sends text messages more frequently.*

2. efficiently   _____

3. effectively   _____

4. badly   _____

5. quickly   _____

6. easily   _____

Avoid Common Mistakes

1 Circle the mistakes.

1. Today, people live **more long**, eat **better**, and exercise **more frequently** than
                                 (a)   (b)   (c)

   100 years ago.

2. Transportation is **more comfortable**, **more efficient**, and **more faster** than in the past.
                                (a)   (b)   (c)

3. Ben wrote a **more better** report than Tom did. It was **more interesting** and **easier** to read.
                      (a)   (b)   (c)

4. This class is **better** than the last. The teacher **is seriouser**, but the subject is **more interesting**.
                 (a)   (b)   (c)

5. My sister goes to bed **earlier than I do**. She also works **harder** and exercises **frequentlier**.
                              (a)   (b)   (c)

6. These days, pollution is **more worse**, the Earth is **warmer**, and the oceans are **dirtier**.
                                (a)   (b)   (c)

7. Today, students study **more long**, use technology **more effectively**, and prepare
                                (a)   (b)

   more carefully.
     (c)

8. Cars are **faster** and **more efficient than** before. They're also **more comfortable then**
             (a)   (b)   (c)

   20 years ago.

2 Read Becky's e-mail to her friend who moved away 15 years ago. Find and correct eight more mistakes.

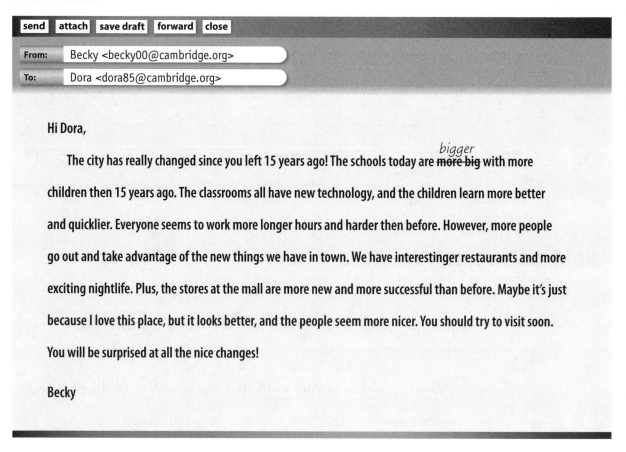

send attach save draft forward close

From: Becky <becky00@cambridge.org>

To: Dora <dora85@cambridge.org>

Hi Dora,

The city has really changed since you left 15 years ago! The schools today are ~~more big~~ *bigger* with more

children then 15 years ago. The classrooms all have new technology, and the children learn more better

and quicklier. Everyone seems to work more longer hours and harder then before. However, more people

go out and take advantage of the new things we have in town. We have interestinger restaurants and more

exciting nightlife. Plus, the stores at the mall are more new and more successful than before. Maybe it's just

because I love this place, but it looks better, and the people seem more nicer. You should try to visit soon.

You will be surprised at all the nice changes!

Becky

Self-Assessment

Circle the word or phrase that correctly completes each sentence.

1. Global communication today is _____ than before.

   a. better   b. gooder   c. more better

2. My new car is _____ than my old car.

   a. comfortabler   b. more comfortable   c. comfortable

3. Today people travel more frequently _____ in the past.

   a. that   b. than   c. then

4. Environmental problems are _____ than they were 100 years ago.

   a. more worse   b. bad   c. worse

5. Most homes today have _____ electrical appliances than before.

   a. energy-efficienter   b. more energy-efficient   c. energy-efficient

6. Mark speaks Spanish _____ since he started working for a Spanish corporation.

   a. more fluently   b. fluentier   c. more fluent

7. In the past, computers were _____ .

   a. more big and heavier   b. bigger and more heavier   c. bigger and heavier

8. There are narrow roads in the city, but there are _____ roads in the suburbs.

   a. wider   b. more wider   c. more narrower

9. When we were in college, Susan studied harder _____ I did.

   a. than   b. that   c. then

10. John listens _____ than his brother does.

    a. carefullier   b. more carefully   c. more careful

11. I can swim _____ than the other swimmers on the team.

    a. furtherly   b. more further   c. further

12. My home is _____ since my son got married.

    a. more quiet   b. more quietly   c. quieter

13. They are constructing this house _____ than my house.

    a. more slowly   b. slower   c. more slow

14. The big cities today are _____ than they were 50 years ago.

    a. more congesteder   b. congested   c. more congested

15. Today, people are _____ than they were 100 years ago.

    a. more taller   b. more tall   c. taller

Superlative Adjectives and Adverbs

Facts and Opinions

Superlative Adjectives

1 Read the sentences about weather facts. Write the superlative form of the adjectives in parentheses.

1. The _greatest_ (great) snowfall from a single storm was 189 inches (480 centimeters) at Mount Shasta in California.

2. The _____ (high) temperature on Earth was 136°F (57.7°C) in Libya.

3. The _____ (low) temperature on Earth was −129°F (−89°C) in Antarctica.

4. The _____ (dry) place on Earth is the Atacama Desert in South America. It has only 0.04 inches (1 millimeter) of rain each year.

5. The _____ (sunny) place in the world is Yuma, Arizona. It is sunny 308 days a year.

6. The _____ (violent) storm was the 1970 Bhola Cyclone in Bangladesh.

7. The _____ (destructive) hurricane in the United States was Hurricane Ike in 1900.

8. The _____ (strong) wind on Earth was 253 miles (408 kilometers) per hour during Cyclone Olivia on Barrow Island, Australia.

9. The _____ (long) rainbow on Earth lasted six hours in Wetherby, England.

10. The _____ (hot) town on Earth is Dallol, Ethiopia. Its average temperature is 94°F (34.4°C).

11. The _____ (cold) town on Earth is Oymyakon, Russia. Its average high temperature is 16.7°F (−8.5°C).

12. The _____ (wet) country on Earth is India with 474 inches (1,204 centimeters) of rain in a year.

2 Complete the conversation with the superlative form of the adjectives in parentheses. Use *the* when necessary. Replace *not* with *least*.

Juan: I know you have a lot of classes this semester. Which is your <u>*most interesting*</u> (1) (interesting) class?

Tony: Well, it's my calculus class. It's my _____ (2) (good) class because I love math. However, it's also my _____ (3) (difficult) class.

Juan: My _____ (4) (hard) class is economics.

Tony: Oh, I'm in that class with you. Who do you think is _____ (5) (intelligent) student in that class?

Juan: Katie is _____ (6) (smart) student in economics. She can answer _____ (7) (complicated) questions that the teacher asks us.

Tony: What is your _____ (8) (not / interesting) class?

Juan: That's easy. It's my history class. I don't like history.

Tony: Which is your _____ (9) (easy) class?

Juan: It's English. I know it's not easy for some students, but for me, it's no problem. Plus, we have _____ (10) (nice) and _____ (11) (patient) professor in that class. All the students love her.

Tony: My biology professor is my favorite. She is _____ (12) (young) professor I have. Biology is my _____ (13) (important) class. I want to go to medical school someday.

3 Write sentences about famous bodies of water. Use the superlative form of the adjectives given.

1. tall / waterfall / in the world / Angel Falls.

   The tallest waterfall in the world is
   Angel Falls.

2. low / sea / in the world / the Dead Sea

   _____

   _____

3. high / lake / in the world / Lake Titicaca

   _____

   _____

4. large / freshwater lake / in the world / Lake Superior

   _____

5. deep / point / in the oceans / the Mariana Trench

   _____

6. long / river / in the world / the Nile River

   _____

7. famous / river / in China / the Yangtze River

   _____

8. salty / body of water / in the United States / the Great Salt Lake

   _____

9. dangerous / river / in South America / the Amazon River

   _____

10. small / sea / in the world / the Sea of Marmara

    _____

11. old / lake / in the world / Lake Baikal

    _____

12. powerful / waterfall / in North America / Niagara Falls

    _____

4 Write sentences about a country you know well using the noun and the superlative form of the adjectives given. Use your own opinion. Use *the most* or *the least* with two- or three-syllable superlatives.

1. popular sport   *The most popular sport in my country is soccer.* _____

2. delicious food   _____

3. popular music   _____

4. good university   _____

5. important person   _____

6. tall building   _____

Superlative Adverbs

1 Complete the sentences below with the superlative form of the adverbs in parentheses.

1. Kayo works _(the) hardest_ (hard) in her office.

2. She concentrates _____ (intensely) of all the employees.

3. She arrives _____ (early) of all the employees.

4. She types _____ (accurately) of all the employees.

5. She does _____ (well) she can in everything.

6. Carl gets to work _____ (late) of all the employees.

7. He takes breaks _____ (frequently) of all employees.

8. He sits _____ (far) away from the windows.

9. He started his job _____ (recently) of all the employees.

10. Their manager supervises his team _____ (effectively) of all the managers at the company.

11. He explains the work _____ (clearly) of all the managers.

12. He treats his team _____ (respectfully) of all the managers.

2 Complete the conversations with the superlative form of the adverbs in parentheses.

A Dana: I think we did well in the tryouts for the college musical yesterday. You danced

(the) most gracefully (gracefully) of all the dancers. You are very talented.
   (1)

Tim: Thanks, Dana. And you sang _____ (well) of all the
                                       (2)

singers. You have a beautiful voice.

Dana: Thanks, Tim. Unfortunately, Tina had a bad day. She sang

_____ (badly) of everyone.
(3)

Tim: That was a shame, but the actors were very good. I think Yolanda acted

_____ (convincingly) for her part. However, Majid
(4)

didn't do as well. He performed _____ (nervously) of all
(5)

the actors.

B Luís: I think the engineering students work _____ (hard) of all
(6)

the students on this campus.

Jenn: Yes, I agree. We arrive on campus _____ (early), and we
(7)

leave _____ (late). We study all the time.
(8)

Luís: The good thing is that the engineering professors teach

_____ (effectively) because they explain the material
(9)

_____ (clear) of all the teachers on campus. I usually
(10)

understand everything.

Jenn: You're right. I'm glad we're engineering students.

3 Write the questions and answers. Use the superlative form of the adverbs given. Replace *not* with *least*.

1. which / continent / is growing / fast

   Q: *Which continent is growing (the) fastest?* _____

   A: *Asia is growing (the) fastest.* _____ (Asia)

2. which / big country / is growing / slowly

   Q: _____

   A: _____ (Russia)

3. which country / lies / far / from the Equator

   Q: _____

   A: _____ (Iceland)

4. which country / hosts / visitors / frequently

   Q: _____

   A: _____ (France)

5. which continent / gets / visitors / not often

   Q: _____

   A: _____ (Antarctica)

6. which country in Europe / educates students / effectively

   Q: _____

   A: _____ (Finland)

4 Write sentences about some of the people in your class. Use superlative adverbs. Replace *not* with *least*.

1. study / hard   *Marcia studies hardest.* _____

2. speak / quietly   _____

3. talk / loudly   _____

4. write / well   _____

5. arrive / late   _____

6. ask questions / not frequent   _____

Avoid Common Mistakes

1 Circle the mistakes.

1. Of all my friends, Maria is (smarter). She gets **the best grades**, and she is
      (a)   (b)

   the **hardest worker**.
      (c)

2. Ho Chi Minh City is **the biggest** and **the busyest** city in Vietnam, but not
                       (a)   (b)

   the most historic.
       (c)

3. Brian studies **the hardest**. Rita studies **the most long**. José gets **the best** grades.
                    (a)   (b)   (c)

4. Asad is **the tallest** student, James is **the shortest** student, and Rob is
              (a)   (b)

   the most strongest.
        (c)

5. China is **the largest country of the world**. Chile is **the longest**, and Vatican City is
               (a)   (b)

   the smallest.
       (c)

6. My class is **the quietest**. Pablo's class is **the loudest**, and Kim's class is **the most smart**.
                  (a)   (b)   (c)

7. Mr. Jones's voice is **the loudest**. Dr. Park's voice is **the softer**, Dr. Ruiz's voice is
   (a)$$(b)

   the clearest.
   (c)

8. Main Street is **the most widest** street. Central Street is **the narrowest**, and 5th Street is
   (a)(b)

   the dirtiest.
   (c)

2 Read part of a student's report on Venezuela. Find and correct eight more mistakes.

prettiest

Venezuela is a beautiful country in South America. It has some of the ~~prettyest~~ geography in South America. It has the tallest waterfall of the world. Angel Falls is over 3,200 feet high.

The bigest city in Venezuela is Caracas, the nation's capital. It's also the most important city. Venezuela has the most richest oil reserves in South America. It exports oil to many countries. The higher point in the country is Pico Bolívar in the state of Merida. It has snow at all times of the year.

Venezuela has many strange animals, but the most strange animal is the capybara. It is the largest rodent of the world. The country has a tropical climate. The rainyest part of the year is from May to November. The most cool part of the country is in the mountains, and the hottest part is along the beaches.

Self-Assessment

Circle the word or phrase that correctly completes each sentence.

1. The red diamond is _____ gem in the world.

   a. the rarest   b. the most rarest   c. the rarer

2. Kyle gets _____ grades of all the students in his class.

   a. the goodest   b. the most good   c. the best

3. Yuko arrived _____ in the United States of all her classmates.

   a. most recent   b. most recently   c. recentliest

4. Which printer copies _____ ?

    a. faster   b. fast   c. fastest

5. _____ item on the menu is a sandwich.

    a. The least expensivest   b. Least expensive   c. The least expensive

6. Paola types _____ of all her classmates.

    a. more accurate   b. most accurate   c. most accurately

7. My father is _____ businessman I know.

    a. the most success   b. the most successful   c. the successfulest

8. Which is _____ metal on earth?

    a. the heavyest   b. the most heavy   c. the heaviest

9. Amber is the lightest gemstone _____ .

    a. in the world   b. of the world   c. than the world

10. Lisa can hit a ball _____ of all the members on her baseball team.

    a. farthest   b. most far   c. farther

11. I think Venice Beach is the most _____ beach in all of California.

    a. beautifully   b. beautifullest   c. beautiful

12. _____ country in the world is Vatican City.

    a. The tiniest   b. The tinyest   c. The most tiny

13. Of all the students in class, Rex always sits _____ to the teacher.

    a. closest   b. most close   c. closer

14. _____ street in my town is Mint Street.

    a. The least congested   b. Least congested   c. The least congestedly

15. Adam jumps _____ of all the members of his basketball team.

    a. most high   b. most highest   c. highest